GUY MARY-ROUSSELIÈRE
1913 — 1994

Charles Choque, O.M.I.

Du même auteur — By the same Author (Charles Choque, o.m.i.)

Biographies:

Kayoaluk, Pierre Henry, o.m.i., Apôtre des Inuit — Édition française 1982, (épuisée).

Kajualuk, Pierre Henry, o.m.i., Apostle of the Inuit — English Edition 1985, 285 pages.

Joseph Buliard, o.m.i., Pêcheur d'Hommes — Édition française 1985, 264 pages.

Joseph Buliard, o.m.i., Fisher of Men — English Edition 1987, 260 pages.

Mikilar, Lionel Ducharme, o.m.i. — Édition française 1992, 230 pages.

Mikilar, Lionel Ducharme, o.m.i. — English Edition 1992, 230 pages.

*	En vente au:	Musée Eskimo, B.P. 10, Churchill, Manitoba, R0B 0E0, Canada.
	Available from:	Eskimo Museum, Box 10, Churchill, Manitoba, R0B 0E0, Canada.

Monographies — Monographs:

L'Hôpital Ste-Thérèse, St. Thérèse Hospital — Chesterfield Inlet, NWT (English and French in one booklet).

75ᵉ anniversaire de la Première Mission Catholique chez les Inuit de la Baie d'Hudson (1987) (French only).

Notices nécrologiques — Obituaries:

Marc Lacroix (1906-1976)
Pierre Henry (1904-1976)
Lionel Ducharme (1899-1979)
Omer Robidoux (1913-1986)
Eugène Fafard (1902-1987)
Jacques Volant (1900-1987)
Julien-Marie Cochard (1907-1990)
André Steinmann (1912-1991)
Hubert Mascaret (1913-1991)
Marcel Rio (1899-1992)
Ernest Trinel (1918-1993)

GUY
MARY-ROUSSELIÈRE
1913 — 1994

Charles Choque, O.M.I.

MÉDIASPAUL

Phototypesetting: *Médiaspaul*

Photos: *Churchill Hudson Bay Diocese Archives*

Cover: *Summum*

Legal Deposit — 4rd Quarter 1998
Bibliothèque nationale du Québec
National Library of Canada

ISBN 0-9692163-5-1 (R.C. Ep. Corp. Churchill)

© 1998 R.C. Episcopal Corporation
            Churchill, Manitoba, Canada

            Médiaspaul
            3965, boul. Henri-Bourassa Est
            Montréal, QC, H1H 1L1 (Canada)

TABLE OF CONTENTS

Dear Readers,

ESKIMO N.S. Nᵒ.47-48, Fall-Winter 1994-1995, the official magazine of the Churchill-Hudson-Bay Diocese, announced the tragic death of Father Guy Mary-Rousselière. Later in an article of ESKIMO N.S. Nᵒ.49, Spring-Summer 1995, with great respect and affection for a well-loved confrère, I summarized his life, his personality and his scientific work. I also mentioned that in order to draw a more conclusive portrait of Father Guy, a book should be written. I now have the pleasure of presenting you with this book which has no scholarly ambition but claims to be only a humble biography where the devoted missionary priest, the unfailing friend of the Inuit, and the renowned archaeologist merge in one portrait profoundly attractive because profoundly human. My deepest gratitude goes first to Father Mary-Rousselière himself whose literary production was unlimited, secondly to his family, to his faithful friends, to the Oblate missionaries and to all my collaborators[1] who did help me to kindle in the arctic sky one more northern light.

Charles Choque,o.m.i.

175 Main Street
Ottawa, Ontario, Canada, K1S 1C3
Telephone: (613) 237-0580 — Facsimile: (613) 232-4064

[1] Sr. Jeannette Fontaine, s.j.a., who translated the French text into English, working graciously without retribution; Colly Scullion, a devoted friend of Father Mary and of the Pond Inlet people, who proofread the English version; Lorraine Brandson, curator of the Eskimo Museum in Churchill, for many constructive suggestions and most of the photographs illustrating the biography; Susan Marsh who, with speed and accuracy, put the whole work on computer; Reynald Rouleau, o.m.i., Bishop of Churchill-Hudson Bay, for his friendship, his encouragement and his financial help.

7

PREFACE

I have always been fascinated by the Polar Regions. When I was a boy, I was surrounded by numerous souvenirs of the Antarctic and Arctic scientific expeditions commanded by my grandfather Captain Adrien de Gerlache de Gomery. Later I witnessed the preparations made by my father for the Belgian expeditions to the Antarctic since 1957.

When I was eleven years old, in 1961, my father took us, my mother, my oldest brother and myself, on board a Danish icebreaker to the East coast of Greenland. That is when I got my first attack of arctic fever.

A few years later, in 1966, we welcomed into our home an Oblate missionary who was holidaying in Belgium. He had a long black beard and had been in the Canadian Arctic for thirty years among the Inuit of Pelly Bay. Like them, he dressed in an outfit made of caribou skin, very warm but cumbersome. He had heard about the modern equipment of the Belgian expeditions to the other end of the world, and he was interested in comparing both. This encounter was the first of the many contacts we had with Father Vandevelde in the years to come.

In the spring of 1973, to my great joy, Father Vandevelde mentioned to his fellow Oblate and good friend Guy Mary-Rousselière that I was willing to be his assistant for the coming summer archaeological excavations at

Nunguvik, a historical site situated a couple hundred miles from Pond Inlet, his parish.

Father Mary accepted my offer and on the 7th of July, I landed in the most northern settlement of Baffin Land and met Ataata Mari, as he was called by his Eskimo friends.

We were to meet again in the Arctic in 1975 and 1977 and several times in Europe. My brother François and my two sisters Henrianne and Hélène were also given the opportunity to become his archaeological assistants. We were privileged each in turn to make the acquaintance of a very extraordinary man, totally faithful to his God and to his missionary calling. He was very close to his family, especially to his sister Béatrice, to his Seminary and Oblate confrères and friends, keeping them all in his heart.

During the few weeks we spent together in a tent at Nunguvik or in the mission at Pond Inlet, many times I heard him making mention of his friends, scientists or not, like Graham Rowley, John Scullion, André Leroi-Gourhan, Jørgen Meldgaard, Doug Heyland, Desmond Sparham, Hermann Steltner... and many others. He did also take great pleasure in recalling his own funny adventures resulting from his legendary absent-mindedness!

Father Mary-Rousselière was a scientist of high cali- bre, devoting his priestly ideal and his knowledge to the service of men, the Inuit. His investigations and his discoveries did help solve many enigmas and gave us precious information on the arctic civilizations. His work, the articles he wrote in the *Eskimo* and his films are great documents to enable the Inuit to re-discover their roots. Because of him, they will also unearth objects such as blades made of flint, harpoon heads, bows and arrows, knives, scra- pers or masks, figurines and even skis made by their predecessors.

They will also learn the string-games of the Arviligjuarmiut, the history of a migration to the North-West of Greenland, the saga of the Queen of Igloolik or other celebrities of the Canadian Arctic.

May I be allowed here to express my sincere gratitude to Father Charles Choque, o.m.i. who is giving us this lively biography of Ataata Mary, the generous priest from the top of the world. The reader will come to know many interesting pieces of information on the Great North, its inhabitants and on the dedicated work of the Oblate Missionaries.

May I be allowed also to call on my friend Nutarak, a true Inuk who came to dig with us at Nunguvik, Saatut and Arnakadlak, and to say together: "Kuyannamik Ataata Mari! Thank you for everything you handed down to us!"

If one day you visit Pond Inlet, please stop at the Mission and admire the painting behind the altar. It comes from the old historic church. The artist is no other than Ataata Mari. It will make you understand everything!

Jean-Louis de Gerlache de Gomery,

Brussels, January 1998

Photo of the Guy Mary-Rousselière painting (Pond Inlet Mission)

1

CHILDHOOD AND VOCATION

Guy Henri Marie Louis was born in Le Mans, in the department of la Sarthe, France, on July 6, 1913. His father, René Mary-Rousselière following in the footsteps of his grandfather and two great-grandfathers, was a pharmacist and died of a disease he contracted when in mandatory service, in November 1918 at the end of the First World War.

The genealogical tree of the Mary-Rousselière family goes back to Sir Etienne-Marie de la Rousselière, a textile merchant in Laval, a member of the Avesnières parish who was buried in the local cemetery in 1719 where his father Etienne-Marie de la Davière had also been interned in 1691. The sons of the latter took the name of certain farms and family properties. Among these, Etienne-Marie, the merchant, who was, from that time forward, known as Etienne-Marie de la Rousselière. It was the time when families had many children. Etienne-Marie, married to Louise-Aimée Bouchard de la Reynière, daughter of a King's Counsellor, sired fifteen children. One of his descendants, Jean Léonard Marie, was baptized on the 22nd of February 1748 by l'abbé Desprey. His godfather was Mathurin Mary, Sieur de la Rousselière. Jean Léonard begot Florent Mary de la Rousselière, husband of Renée le Bailleul. Florent and Renée had among their offspring a son, René Vital Florent Mary de la Rousselière who became a pharmacist and was Emile Mary-Rousselière's father, the great-grandfather of the missionary.

While flipping through the parochial registers or the departmental archives of yore, it is evident that the family name was often spelled differently: Marie, Mary, Mari or even Marye. It seems that the Marie de la Rousselière family belonged to the middle class; they were tradesmen who migrated to St. Denis du Maine at the dawn of the XVIIIth century. Unwilling to mix with the local population, they preferred to contract alliances with families of similar financial conditions who lived in the surrounding areas.

One of the preoccupations of Father Guy Mary-Rousselière on his last visits to France was to locate exactly the place known as "La Rousselière". He worshipped his ancestors and no doubt, in his demeanour, he showed some of their nobility.

He spent a happy childhood at Le Mans, a childhood which was however somewhat darkened by the accidental death, August 12, 1917, of his brother Bernard, his junior by twenty months. Bernard had fallen down the stairs, head first, and had died of meningitis a short time later.

In 1919, after her husband's death, Mrs. Mary-Rousselière, born Yvonne Le Cardonnel, distressed by her recent widowhood, holding the hands of young Guy and his sister Béatrice, his senior by four years, moved to Paris close to her next-of-kin. In spite of the affectionate presence of his maternal grandparents, Guy felt very restrained in a city apartment. He yearned for the large gardens of Le Mans where as a little boy he ran and played. He missed the Saint Joseph School where he learned to read and write, to draw and sing.

In Paris, he went to the private school kept by the Demoiselles Poupon. Besides the school manuals, each pupil had to own a hoop to be played with during the daily recreation periods spent in the Luxembourg public garden.

In 1920, still in Paris, he enrolled at St. Francis-Xavier parochial school but not for long. His mother finding him a little too mischievous, sent him to the Notre Dame Institution at Saint Calais in the Sarthe, hoping that the Superior, who was somewhat related to her family, could redress her son's difficult character. When the time arrived for his mother to leave him, the little boy did not show any special sorrow but at night, when alone in his bed, he wept profusely. The school discipline was very strict. Any little infringement to the regulations was severely punished by a slap on the face. In that particular region, winters are bitterly cold, and little Guy suffered from painful chilblains. Still, he did enjoy his stay at Saint Calais and true friendships which lasted all his life bound him to some of his schoolmates. He remained there from 1922 to 1925, then went back to Paris to continue his secondary studies at the Fontanes School. He finally graduated at the Seminary of Conflans, at Charenton-Le-Pont, (Seine).

Guy was an avid reader. The *Annals of the Propagation of the Faith* and a book just published and entitled *Aux Glaces Polaires,* by Father Pierre Duchaussois, o.m.i., laureate of the 1921 "Prix Montyon", offered by the French Academy, awakened in him the desire to become a missionary in the Congregation of the Oblates of Mary Immaculate. The lectures given by Bishop Grouard[1], an old long white bearded pioneer of imposing stature, intensified his intention to enter the priesthood.

But first, before joining the Oblates, he registered at the Saint Sulpice Seminary at Issy-les-Moulineaux, southwest

---

[1] Emile GROUARD, French Oblate, cousin of Bishop Vital Grandin, Apostolic Vicar of Athabasca-Mackenzie, deceased in Grouard, Alberta, in 1931.

of Paris. Here he completed his studies in philosophy and was given a good start in theology. On June 10, 1933, he received the tonsure, the first visible sign of the clerical state, a rite which has been more or less forgotten since Vatican II.

In 1933, he interrupted his studies to enlist for mandatory military service. He declined the offer to be sent to Morocco, unwilling to be separated from his mother. He joined the army at Mourmelon-le-Grand in the Marne and later at Châlons. The lack of hygiene in the sanitary facilities installed out of doors was appalling. He had to go outside to wash himself in freezing water. During the winter, the cold was so severe that the wolves were coming out of the forests to scavenge for food. In the barracks, the coal stoves were throwing so little heat that the windows were covered with frost. As it was strictly forbidden to wear gloves during the military exercises, chilblains reappeared! Guy became sick and was sent to the infirmary. The Colonel of the 8th Zouaves to which he belonged, finding him too thin, ordered for him a supplementary ration. In October 1934, at the end of his assignment, he left the camp of Châlons. The Chaplain, Franciscan Dominique-M. Jourdain, would then testify that Chief Corporal Guy Mary-Rousselière had given proof of irreproachable conduct during his year of military service, always ready to help in the ministry in favour of soldiers or to direct singing during ceremonies in the military chapel.

Notwithstanding the risks inherent to military life, Guy kept intact his desire to become a missionary. No sooner had he left the uniform, he requested his admission among the Oblates of Mary Immaculate.This Congregation had been founded, January 25, 1816, by Charles Joseph Eugene de Mazenod, Bishop of Marseille, whose sainthood was officially declared by Pope Jean-Paul II, December 3, 1995. Guy's mother did not object to her son becoming a missionary, for she herself had advised the Master of Novices, Father Joseph Pitard (1875-1941) of his decision. At that time, in order to conform to article 545 of Canon Law, the candidates to religious life had to obtain permission from their bishops to leave the diocese before registering in the congregation of their choice. In the fall of 1934, provided with the *Nihil Obstat* of Cardinal Verdier, Archbishop of Paris, he entered the Oblate novitiate at Berder. Built on an islet in the Gulf of Morbihan, this former château was entirely surrounded by well-kept lawns and magnificent trees. On October 31, 1934, Guy donned the long, black cassock of the Oblates and became *Brother* Mary-Rousselière. During the twelve months of the noviti-ate, he willingly accepted to be cast in the mould of religious life. He was faithful to its obligations and duties, sweeping corridors, washing dishes, shaking sand fleas from the bed sheets, raking paths in the park or spending many hours of prayer and meditation in the chapel before the Blessed Sacrament; thus learning to renounce his own will in order to accept more readily God's will. Here at Berder, he formed a solid friendship with Joseph and Robert Buliard, both native of Le Barboux, a little hamlet in Franche-Comté. Joseph[2] was later sent to the Canadian North and, in 1956, he disappeared in the Garry Lake country. Robert, Joseph's cousin, is still a missionary at Notre Dame of Sion.

Following a year of probation, spent in an atmosphere of silence, reflection, work and prayer, on November 1, 1935, "Vitus"[3] Mary-Rousselière took the vows of poverty,

---

[2] For more details on Joseph Buliard, see his biography: *Joseph Buliard, Fisher of Men,* by Charles Choque, available from the Eskimo Museum, Box 10, Churchill, Manitoba, R0B 0E0, Canada.

[3] Vitus is the latin name for Guy.

chastity and obedience for one year. The Novice Master's report described him as an impulsive temperament, physically in very good health and suited to any climate. His behaviour was very correct, but his apparent timidity made him a bit awkward and withdrawn. Intellectually, the report confirmed what the Superior of the Seminary of Issy had

said of him: "A regular student capable to succeed in all subjects." He possessed or at least cultivated satisfactorily all moral qualities, such as charity, piety, spirit of faith, in short, all the supernatural virtues required by his vocation. Nothing transcendent but, concluded the report, he was cut out to be an *ordinary* subject. The word "ordinary" greatly surprises when we know what he did accomplish during his life!

From 1935 to 1938, as a member of the French Northern Oblate Province, Brother Mary-Rousselière studied theology at the Seminary of the Missions at La-Brosse-Montceaux, in Latin "Bruscia-Moncelli", a name fit for a former château situated in the centre of a magnificent park on the Paris-Sens route. A skilful confrère, thoughtful, of sound judgement, he was also remarkable for his singing talents and his skill as a caricaturist.

Guy Mary-Rousselière,
young priest, c. 1937

In March 1936, he received, as was the custom then in the Roman Catholic Church, the four minor orders making him porter, lector, acolyte and exorcist. An indult received from Rome, authorized him to advance the date of his perpetual vows to the 8th of December, 1937. At this time he received the Oblate cross that he wore proudly at the waist and which he cherished all his life until the moment when, like himself, it would be half consumed by the fire that destroyed the mission of Pond Inlet on April 23, 1994. On the 18th of that same December 1937, after receiving at very short intervals the major orders of subdiaconate and diaconate, he was ordained to the priesthood in the church of La Brosse-Montceaux by Monseigneur Jules Cenez, o.m.i., first Apostolic Vicar of Basutoland (today, Lesotho, Central Africa). A disciple of the Blessed Father Gérard, apostle of the Basutos, Monseigneur Cenez resigned for health reasons in 1930 and retired to Notre Dame of Sion. He died on March 2, 1944.

Father Guy Mary-Rousselière was prepared to go and work in Africa, for example, in the Apostolic Vicariate of Windhoeck in Namibia, or anywhere in Asia, particularly in Laos, or in South America, perhaps along the Pilcomayo. Nevertheless, his preference—and he does not hide it in a letter to his Superior General, dated November 28, 1937—was for the Canadian North with the Eskimos, better known today as Inuit. But there was always the possibility that his superiors would keep him in France as a professor at the Juniorate, he has knowledge, is a good organizer, sings and draws well, or as a preacher taking part in popular missions, his style is elegant and sober. In brief, he is a very good subject, concluded the official report drafted in view of his first obedience, a subject who would be precious to his Oblate province of origin and excellent for the foreign missions. A subject, after all, not so "ordinary" as was once mentioned. His health was robust enough to adapt to any climate. His ability to adjust with ease to the mentality and temperament of the natives was remarkable. At Saint Sulpice, without any difficulty, he had been in contact with many foreigners, particularly students of Chinese and Japanese descent.

In 1936, Monseigneur Arsène Turquetil, a French Oblate, the first Apostolic Vicar of the Hudson Bay missions, was in Holland to supervise the construction of a boat made of steel, strong enough to defy the arctic ice. He would name her the *M. F. Therese*, in honour of his compatriot, the little Saint of Lisieux, whose heavenly power obtained the first Eskimo conversions at Chesterfield Inlet in 1917. Bishop Turquetil visited La Brosse-Montceaux and celebrated Christmas there with the scholastics, captivating them with tales of hard northern trips by dogteam, cold nights spent in igloos and frightening encounters with shamans covered with amulets.

For the most beautiful, the most difficult, the most meritorious mission in the world, according to Pope Pius XI, Monseigneur Turquetil needed solid and motivated recruits. He chose amongst the scholastics having completed their studies André Steinmann[4] from La Brosse-Montceaux, Hubert Mascaret[5] from Cineto Romano (Italy) and Joseph Choque[6] from Velaines-lez-Tournai (Belgium). At Marseilles, all together they boarded a ship of the Dreyfuss

---

[4] André Steinmann (1912-1991). He published his autobiography *La Petite Barbe* in 1977, Editions de l'Homme, Montréal. Cf. also *Eskimo* Spring-Summer 1992, an article by Fr. Mary-Rousselière on Fr. Steinmann, 11 pages.

[5] Hubert Mascaret (1913-1991), born in Epinal (France), missionary among the Inuit of New Quebec and Hudson Bay. Died in St Boniface, Manitoba.

[6] Joseph Choque (1912-1979). Oblate born in Belgium, missionary in the North from 1938 to 1979. He ministered mainly to the Inuit of Cape Dorset, Baker Lake, Coral Harbour and Iqaluit. Brother of Charles Choque, o.m.i.

Bishop Arsène Turquetil, o.m.i. Founder of the
Apostolic Vicariate of Hudson Bay. (1876-1955)

M. F. Therese, the mission boat
built in Holland in 1936.

Company, the *Jean L. D.,* heading for Galveston,Texas. They arrived in Montreal just in time to catch the *M. F. Therese* on her way north. Father Steinmann landed at Wakeham Bay, actually Kangiqsujuaq, July 19, 1938; Father Mascaret went to Ivuyivik and Father Joseph Choque to Chesterfield.

Father Mary-Rousselière was first designated to stay in France but was saved from that obedience by the Northern Canadian Bishops who were insistently knocking at the General Administration's door in order to receive new recruits immediately. On July 2, 1938, an official document from Rome, all in Latin, asked him in the name of Holy Obedience to go as soon as possible to the Oblate missions of the Canadian North and more specifically to the Mackenzie Vicariate. However this was soon changed in favour of the Hudson Bay Vicariate. He was to replace Father Roche who, having contracted tuberculosis, was unable to depart. Bishop Breynat of the Mackenzie was disappointed; Bishop Turquetil was jubilant and Father Mary-Rousselière, very happy. He probably expressed his gratitude to Monseigneur Turquetil who was again in 1938 passing through France with Father Lionel Ducharme[7], one of his first arctic missionaries, on their way to Rome. Both had been summoned to attend the 23rd General Chapter of the Congregation in September. Alas! rumours of war brought a premature ending to the meeting.

Both Guy's mother and his sister Béatrice had attended his ordination to the priesthood and the first Mass he celebrated in the chapel of the scholasticate. Now the time had come to say good-bye. However, before his departure in June 1938, at Pontoise, in a church dedicated to

---

[7] Cf. *MIKILAR, Lionel Ducharme, Apostle of the Inuit* by Charles Choque, available, in French or in English, at the Eskimo Museum, Box 10, Churchill, Manitoba, R0B 0E0, Canada.

St. Maclou, now a cathedral, he had the great joy of baptizing his sister's first child, Marie-Renée. Béatrice was married to René Charbonnel. Many years later at Pond Inlet, Marie-Renée and her sister Geneviève, on a cold, pale night in May 1994, will accompany their uncle to his last resting place. Neither long separations nor huge distances, made Father Guy's affection for his family ever dwindle.

2

MISSIONARY IN CANADA

In August 1938, Father Mary-Rousselière went to Le Havre to board the *M. S. Ausonia* ready to set sail for Canada. He was accompanied by an Oblate Brother André Chauvel, (1905-1972), a native of the Atlantic Loire, who was sent to the new mission of Cape Dorset at the southwest bottom of Baffin Land.They arrived too late in Montreal to travel north to the Hudson Bay. The sailing season to the Arctic was over. The *M. F. Therese* had left long ago and was already in Repulse Bay battling against the ice. The *M. S. Nascopie*, the supplier of the Hudson Bay Company trading posts, had already dropped anchors at Chesterfield. At the same time Father Schulte[1] was landing on the bay bringing back in his plane Father Julien-Marie Cochard[2] who had become ill at Arctic Bay.

Disappointed not to continue north, Father Rousselière, —this is how most of the people shortened his name—, took accommodation in Bishop Turquetil's residence, a comfortable house donated by a generous benefactor, situated on

---

[1] Paul Schulte, a German Oblate, has written his adventures as a pilot in *The Flying Priest over the Arctic* (Harper, U.S.A., 1940).

[2] Julien-Marie Cochard (1907-1990), Oblate missionary born in Brittany; worked in the Arctic from 1934 to 1963 before retiring among the Oblates of the Holy Rosary Province (Québec). Cf. *Eskimo* Spring-Summer 1991, a short biography by Charles Choque.

Julien-Marie Cochard, o.m.i. (1907-1990)

Bloomfield Street in Outremont. This house was used to welcome missionaries going north or coming south, needing rest or medical care, such as Father Prime Girard[3] whose eyes had been damaged by the brilliance of the snow;

---

[3] Prime Girard (1883-1949), French Canadian, first joined the Oblates as a lay Brother. Ordained priest in 1929, he was sent to Pond Inlet. Threatened with blindness, he left the North around 1935 for Montreal. He gave lectures and collected donations for the Arctic missions. He died in Lowell (U.S.A.).

Father Arthur Thibert[4] who had heart trouble, and Father Alain Kermel[5], suffering from bad feet.To kill time, Father Rousselière visited the metropolis, getting used to the Canadian way of speaking French and to the English language predominant in stores. He admired the city's historical monuments, its renowned restaurants, its ancient homes and its magnificent churches whose elegant belfries dominated a conglomeration of races and religions.

Monseigneur Turquetil returned from Rome at the beginning of October aboard the *M. S. Normandy*. In a letter written on December 28, 1938, addressed to Father Anthime Desnoyers, a member of the general administration in Rome, Monseigneur confided his first impressions of Father Rousselière. He found him to be a good religious man but too quiet and withdrawn. His intention was to send him, temporarily at least, to a mission in Saskatchewan or Manitoba to familiarize himself with the Indian language before going to Churchill to keep company to Richard Ferron[6] who was alone most of the time.

Father Rousselière left Montreal dressed in an ill-fitted black suit which he had received from Bishop Turquetil. In Ottawa, he attended the solemn mass said in the Cathedral in memory of Pius XI, the Pope of the Missions. Leaving Ottawa, he took the C.N. train to Winnipeg in the company

---

[4] Arthur Thibert (1898-1963), French Canadian priest, spent 20 years as an Oblate in the Hudson Bay missions. Fluent in Inuktitut, he published a Dictionary, a Sunday Missal, several magazines and kept in touch with the Inuit treated in the South for tuberculosis. He died in the St. Joseph Scholasticate of Ottawa. Cf. his obituary in the *Eskimo*, Christmas 1963.

[5] Alain Kermel (1903-1970), arrived from France in 1929 and was sent to Arviat (Eskimo Point). Sick, he had to leave the North in 1937. He died in Sainte-Agathe-des-Monts and was buried in Richelieu.

[6] Richard Ferron (1907-1995), born in the Diocese of Trois-Rivières, sent to Churchill in 1935, secretary to Bishop Turquetil, bursar of the Hudson Bay Vicariate, founder of Arctic Wings, retired part-time in Cap-de-la-Madeleine, part-time in Mexico.

of Bishop Martin Lajeunesse, Bishop of the Keewatin. In Saint Boniface, he stayed a few days at the Oblate Juniorate until re-boarding the train to Prince Albert in Saskatchewan. He was in the mission of L'Ile à la Crosse when Pius XII was elected Pope on March 2, 1939. The building was old, in need of paint and impregnated with the smell of Father Rossignol's[7] pipe. Father Bourbonnais[8] came to pick him up with his horse drawn sleigh to drive him to Buffalo River. On the sleigh was a little house heated by a wooden stove just enough to keep the passengers warm. The horse was perspiring heavily and covered with frost. From time to time, he was given some hay to eat. It was the beginning of spring but it was still very cold.

During the summer, Bishop Lajeunesse visited the missions and invited Father Rousselière to go along. At each stop, the Bishop was welcomed by a burst of gun fire. As soon as he stepped out of the canoe, the Indians came to kiss his ring. With the episcopal visit over, the Bishop and his oarsmen took again to the river. Father Bourbonnais went along. Father Rousselière could not help admiring his imperturbable calm. No flies, no mosquitoes could distract him from reading a book or his breviary, a success he attributed to his constant pipe smoking. Father Rousselière himself tried to smoke the pipe but to no avail, he did not like it!

From Ile à la Crosse, the Bishop and Father Rousselière took the plane to The Pas. This flight of the *Sancta Maria* was probably the last trip Louis Bisson made in the North before joining the Airforce and serving as an instructor during the Second World War.

---

[7] Marius Rossignol (1875-1961), French Oblate, missionary among the Saskatchewan Indians.

[8] Joseph Bourbonnais (1903-1986), Canadian Oblate from the Valleyfield Diocese, missionary among the Saskatchewan Indians. Buried in Richelieu (Québec).

Churchill—Indian Missions

Father Rousselière was anxious to reach Churchill. There was only one train every three weeks from The Pas to Churchill and the trip took three days. The wooden seats were far from comfortable. At each stop announced by steam whistle, according to a well established ritual, Indians, men and women alike, would board the train at one end and walk across all the wagons. On the station platform at Churchill, Father Ferron was patiently waiting for his visitor to arrive.

Father Guy Mary-Rousselière and
an Indian boy at Duck Lake (1941)

Monseigneur Turquetil knew the Indians well. As soon as he reached Canada in 1900, he had been sent by Father Ovide Charlebois, the future bishop of the Apostolic Vicariate of Keewatin, to the Saint Pierre Mission of Reindeer Lake. From there, at least twice, he had penetrated into Eskimo territory until finally, in 1912, he built the first mission among the Inuit, the mission of Our Lady of the Delivrande, at Chesterfield Inlet. In 1925, he had been named Apostolic Prefect of Hudson Bay, then in 1931, Apostolic Vicar of that same territory detached from Keewatin. If his jurisdiction comprised mainly the Inuit missions, the Sacred Congregation of the Faith had nevertheless entrusted to him and his successor, Monseigneur Marc Lacroix[9], the evangelization of the Montagnais (Sayisi Dene) in the Churchill area. Already somewhat in possession of their language, Father Mary-Rousselière was the obvious choice to minister to the Indians!

In the summer of 1940, with the help of Father Prime Girard who had arrived from Montreal to visit a few of the northern missions, he chartered a plane to transport to Caribou Post the materials for the Saint Mary mission at the cost of $250.00 per ton. Father Girard helped to build the small mission and returned to Churchill. Caribou Post is 100 km northwest of Churchill, on Caribou Lake. There, the trading post of the Honourable Hudson Bay Company was not really flourishing and in spring 1941, they moved the store further west to Duck Lake. Father Mary followed the traders to Duck Lake and stayed in a tent while his small

---

[9] Marc Lacroix, born at Saint Simon de Bagot, Quebec, on the 25th of April 1906. As Oblate, he was sent to the Inuit missions in 1934. Ordained Bishop of the Hudson Bay the 22nd of February 1943, with residence in Churchill, Manitoba. In 1968, he resigned and retired among the Oblates at Rougemont, Quebec. He died on September 9, 1976. Cf. *Eskimo* Fall-Winter 1976-1977.

habitation was being built. Monseigneur Turquetil who knew how great a suffering isolation and solitude can bring about, had ordered Father Rousselière to spend part of the winter in Churchill when most of the Indians were away trapping. There were about one hundred men, most of them traditionally belonging to the Church of England. In general, Father Rousselière found the Indians very sympathetic and appreciative of the services that the Catholic missionaries were always ready to offer them. However, just as Father Egenolf[10] who visited them in 1937 thought, he was convinced that there was very little hope of conversion among them. The Catholic Indians of the Nueltin Lake tribe— approximately seven families—were part until then of the Saint Peter Mission at Reindeer Lake. Monseigneur Lajeunesse, Apostolic Vicar of Keewatin, preoccupied with their fate, wanted to send them a missionary. Father Rousselière went to visit them, doing more ministry on these trips than he did for the rest of the year at Duck Lake. He ventured as far as Windy Lake where there was also a trading post that would soon be closed and where the Inuit living alongside the Kazan River brought their pelts.

In his report to Bishop Lacroix, Father Rousselière again told him that he would willingly go to an Eskimo mission. He also acknowledged that Brother Volant[11], his companion, had helped him enormously with the daily chores, cutting firewood, hunting partridges, cooking meals and yet, in spite of that, he would prefer to live alone, because between him and the Brother "diplomatic relations" were

---

[10] Joseph Egenolf, German Oblate born in 1876, the Canadian West in 1903. Missionary at Reindeer Lake from 1905 until his death at The Pas, Manitoba, March 14, 1957.

[11] Brother Jacques Volant (1900-1987), from Brittany, France. Sent to various missions up North before landing in Churchill in 1940. Known under the name of PIKU, he became the curator of the Eskimo Museum in Churchill.

Brother Jacques Volant

at times a little strained. The Brother was an excellent shot but too easily excitable and one day when hunting caribou the bullet whisked along the ears of his superior! At Duck Lake, at the very onset of winter the caribou were plentiful, providing meat and skins for the people and food for the dogs. A tractor from Churchill carrying merchandise for the trading post, on its way back brought six bundles of skins to be sent to the Northern missions that were short of caribou fur and a pair of well made beaver mittens for Bishop Lacroix, a gift from a Montagnais.

The Bishop not only thought of recalling Brother Volant from Duck Lake but also Father Rousselière whom he wanted to send to Pond Inlet. This was an obedience which pleased Father Rousselière very much but at the same time it made him very anxious for the future of the Indians of the Saint Mary Mission. In June 1944, he informed Monseigneur Martin Lajeunesse, the Bishop of the Keewatin, of his impending departure from Duck Lake, assuring His Excellency of his prayers for the conversion of the Indians under his care.

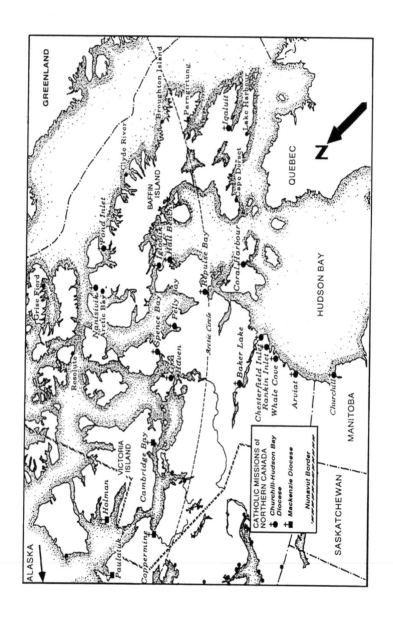

CATHOLIC MISSIONS of NORTHERN CANADA
● Churchill-Hudson Bay Diocese
✚ Mackenzie Diocese
~~~ Nunavut Border

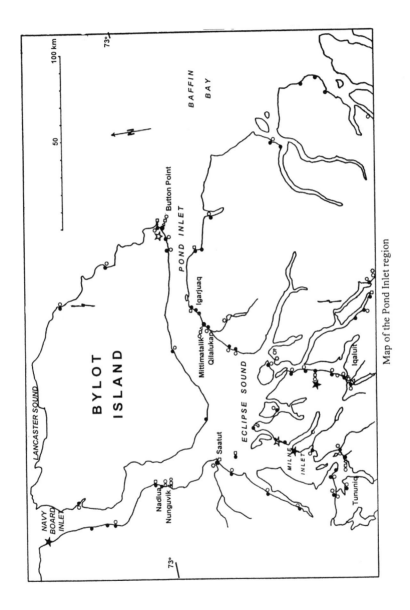

Map of the Pond Inlet region

35

3

POND INLET

Before following Father Guy Mary-Rousselière to Pond Inlet, it would probably be interesting to familiarize the reader with this Inuk settlement as it existed in the 1930's. Etienne Danielo[1], one of the first Oblates to live in this remote village, will be our guide. Just before the arrival of the *M. S. Nascopie*, September 3, 1936, the same boat that Father Rousselière boarded in 1944, he described briefly, for the benefit of his relatives and friends, the scenery, the animal life, the vegetation and the inhabitants of the region.

The Country

Pond Inlet—formerly written Ponds Inlet—owes its name to John Pond, an eminent British astronomer, a contemporary of the John Ross expedition in 1888, and is situated at 72° 41'N, 78°00W', north of Baffin Land, about 700 km north of the Polar Circle, in a country of ice and snow. The scenery is magnificent. The Catholic mission

---

[1] Father Etienne Danielo (1910-1965), French Oblate, studied in Belgium and Italy, spent 20 years at Pond Inlet. After a few more years in Igloolik, Churchill and Chesterfield, his health forced him to retire and in 1964, he came to the Edifice Deschâtelets in Ottawa. He was called "Kayukuluk" by the Inuit. He died Oct.8, 1965 and is buried in Notre Dame cemetery at Hull, Québec.

The Cross on the Hill behind the
R.C. mission in Pond Inlet

Bishop Clabaut and Father Danielo
(Photo M. Flint)

Views of Pond Inlet

Fathers Cochard, Bazin, Danielo and Brother Volant (second on the left)

built on the side of a small hill was founded in the autumn of 1929 by Etienne Bazin[2] and Prime Girard. From its very beginning, it has been surmounted by a large cross. Facing the mission at about 25 km north lies Bylot Island whose interior is one immense icefield from which, with great noise, enormous sections detach themselves in summer, forming huge icebergs drifting away. Some of these icebergs, caught in shallow bays, supply the Inuit with an inexhaustible source of soft water. Eclipse Sound, a vast arm of the sea which rather resembles a large lake and is surrounded by mountains, separates Pond Inlet and Bylot. Because of the almost unlimited visibility due to the flattening of the earth at the polar regions, small mountains can be seen in the west which are more than 150 km away, and many times, we are surprised to walk long hours to reach a goal that seemed so near. This optical illusion gives us time to feel the deep white silence and to admire the wild beauty of a scene that sings so vividly the grandeur of God and the magnificence of his creation.

The Inhabitants

The Inuit call Pond Inlet *Mittimatalik* or the resting place of Mittima, an Inuk whose memory has been perpetuated through the years although remaining vague and imprecise. Ancient tombs, some dating back to more than a thousand years, are the proof that Pond Inlet has long been inhabited. The ground being continually frozen a few centimetres from the surface, the body of the dead wrapped in a caribou skin is placed on top of the ground surrounded by rocks with flat

---

[2] Father Etienne Bazin (1903-1972), French Oblate, famous painter, missionary at Pond Inlet, Igloolik and Repulse Bay. Left the North in 1948 and took the parish of Gorgoloin, in the Diocese of Lyon, his native country. Cf. *Les lettres d'Oncle Etienne* published in 1974 by his nephew.

stones as a cover to protect it from the voracity of dogs, wolves or foxes.

Actually—we are in 1936 and it is still Father Danielo writing—Pond Inlet is a small northern capital with eight white men, two missions, Catholic and Anglican, a HBC trading post and a detachment of the Royal Canadian Mounted Police.

Pond Inlet—RCMP

Many Inuit have deserted Pond Inlet these last years to establish themselves near Arctic Bay or Admiralty Inlet, more than 200 km to the west and northwest. At the post, there were, during winter, only two families engaged by the Royal Canadian Mounted Police. In the spring, the Inuit come in large numbers to trade their furs and spend two or three weeks at the post. After they leave, it is back to habitual calm and tranquillity.

If the Inuit are so dispersed, it is because life's necessities command it. They must continually move, in search of caribou, fox, seal or fish. That is why there are ordinarily no more than two or three families in the same camp; were there more, they would die of hunger. Only this winter, some went many days without food. A police patrol in the Davis Strait, met a family who was at the threshold of death. The father no longer had the strength to go hunting and the very young children were crying for food. The North is very harsh for its poverty stricken inhabitants whose lives depend on the abundance or the lack of game.

As missionaries, we are in charge of the *Tunnunirmiut* tribe (the people on the back of the earth) the last tribe north. There are still now a dozen families further north on Devon, but they were transported there, a few years ago, by the Hudson Bay Company to trap foxes. Our parish has a much larger surface than Brittany with a population of 300 to 350 souls and is a part of the Apostolic Vicariate of Hudson Bay, the least populated vicariate in the world but seven to eight times the size of France.

The movement of conversion to our religion is still to come. A year before the foundation of the Catholic mission, in 1928, Bishop Anderson of the Church of England, passing through Pond Inlet on the *Nascopie*, called a meeting of all the Eskimos who were at the post, and after a short instruction given through an interpreter, baptized them all. He also made them promise that they would never become Catholic. It is not surprising that when a year later, Fathers Girard and Bazin came to Pond, they found the Inuit very prejudiced against them. Even today (always in 1936), this situation still prevails. During his six years here, Father Girard only baptized a few elders or infants on their deathbed. All we have now is one Catholic Eskimo,

Helene *Ublurear* (the Star), baptized at Igloolik, and the oldest Eskimo woman north of Baffin Land.

The arctic dwellers, formerly called Eskimos or eaters of raw meat, spent the winter in igloos. They are primitive, yes, but intelligent, energetic and nomads by necessity, and will become, little by little, what we call "civilized". Already some who lived near the post built themselves little shelters made of a few old cases. In the middle of a dirty floor, a bleeding seal is thawing, food for man and dog. To appease his hunger, the Inuk cuts a piece of half thawed meat, puts it in his mouth and with his "*pilaut*", a small sharp dagger, simply cuts what hangs from the lips. As a substitute for a napkin, to wipe the greasy hands or even the baby's nose, a partridge's skin is the best thing, and if that is not available, there remains the natural towel, the tongue.

To build a travelling igloo, the Eskimo armed with a "*panak*" or long handle knife with a long blade, carves blocks of snow hardened by the wind and places them in a spiral form all around himself; the last block at the top of the igloo is also installed from the interior, so that the builder is imprisoned in his construction. He then cuts a hole at the bottom of the igloo through which he will exit and through which those who are waiting outside, freezing in the cold, will be able to crawl in. Once the sleeping equipment, the grub and the people are in the igloo, the door is hermetically sealed with a block of snow. A few caribou skins are laid on the snow that will serve as bed. A seal oil lamp, the stone *kudliq*, is lit and tea is made. If the heat becomes so excessive that the snow melts, a simple hole in the roof will assure ventilation. As for the dogs, having been fed walrus meat or fish, they simply coil up in a ball and sleep under the stars. In case some of them become loose during the night, all skin traces, whips and harnesses are stored at the top of the igloo out of their reach.

Winter

Our country is a cold, very cold country, but they say that our lowest weather is more bearable than that of Europe, because it is drier. Ordinarily, lakes and ground start to freeze at the beginning of August. From September to June, the snow transforms the landscape in a white and silent immensity. This summer, water started to flow in the small brook near the mission on June 4. The sea freezes over around October and makes an ideal road for the sleds circulating in all directions. This very winter, the ice of the sea was two metres deep and we could travel on it safely until the beginning of July. The coldest months are December, January and February with temperatures as low as 46° below zero and sometimes colder. As soon as the sun returns, it warms up rapidly. Snow storms are frequent and then we need protection from the piercing wind. Once, walking on the sea, I got caught in a blizzard and I had to walk many kilometres backwards to avoid freezing my face, the only part of the body that is left uncovered when wearing caribou clothing. It is then easy to get lost and freeze to death.

The Polar Night

At the North Pole, there are six months of continuous night followed by six months of light. Pond Inlet which is between the Polar Circle and the North Pole, enjoys the polar night but for only three months. The sun is below our horizon from November 5 until February 5. The night is not a continual deep darkness, because around noon, there is a certain light, a diaphanous light, produced especially by the snow covering the ground, a translucent light comparable to that of a beautiful and clear moonlight. When the weather is bad, we have total obscurity, so much so that even at noon it is impossible to notice whether the ground you are treading upon ascends or descends and if there is a hole in the snow, most of the time, you see it too late. This winter fortunately the sky was often very clear and starry and on Christmas Eve, there was a beautiful aurora borealis, a phenomenon so rare in the sky of Pond and so frequent in Churchill.

During the ninety-two days of the polar night, especially in bad weather, even at noon, we keep a lamp lit all the time in the mission or at least a candle. The obscurity that surrounds us protests loudly that man is made to enjoy light, the light of the sun of course, but also the light of the soul. Oh! how great is our joy when we see the reddish line at the horizon that tells us that the sun still shines and warms with its beautiful rays those we love. When the sun reappears for the first time, everyone hurries to climb the surrounding hills to contemplate it the few minutes that it presents to us only a part of its globe!

Abandoning us in winter, the sun will not leave us during spring and summer; from May to August, it will travel in the sky everyday, passing successively by the four cardinal points. There is nothing more interesting than this period allowing you to go out at any hour day and night, as if it were high noon, and, if you so desire, and there is no polar bear in the vicinity, you can read your newspaper outside at midnight.

The Wildlife

The wildlife is not abundant in our white desert, snow covered for at least nine months of the year. Caribou, so numerous in other parts of the Eskimo country, is almost non-existent here. We can see sporadic small herds 100 km south. On the contrary, this year at least—we are still in 1936—the foxes abound. Their beautiful white fur represents the wealth of the Inuit. They exchange them at the trading post for the "white man's" food as well as for the essential hunting articles such as rifles, bullets, knives etc. Because of his natural improvidence, the Inuk never thinks of putting aside a bit of money.

It is the silent wish of every visitor to the Arctic regions to see a white bear. I admit that I have only seen one young cub captured by the Eskimos and brought to the police. Tracks of polar bears are seen at one time or another on the sea, not far from the post. The sea abounds with marine animals. The seal provides excellent dog food and a gourmet dish for the Inuit. During the winter, it keeps a hole free of ice where it comes up to breathe once in a while. The Eskimo hunter, immobile, awaits it, spear in hand, during long hours, exposed to the wind and intense cold. The narwhals and walruses are not as common but are just as much appreciated for their meat and ivory. The large whales once numerous and hunted for their baleen and their oil have practically disappeared. The whalebones seen on the seashore tell their story and the huge dimensions of this enormous sea mammal. They were used to cover old dwellings made of rocks and sand. Fish, fresh and delicious, is our habitual nourishment, at least during the summer. At the end of June, the Arctic Char comes down to the sea and is caught in our nets. End of August or early September, the char returns to the lakes in the interior of the country and late in autumn and during winter, we catch them with nets or we go jigging under the ice of the lakes.

Geese during spring migration

Caribou

Inuk pulling seal from breathing hole

The Dogs

A medium size dog team will devour two or three thousand fish a year. The dogs are our friends. We probably like them more than Parisian ladies their poodles. Even if we have to be rough with them at times, they remain our inseparable travelling companions even in periods of misery and starvation. We like them primarily because they allow us to visit and give spiritual help to the camps and to take care of the sick. An average team here is made of ten or twelve dogs although poor hunters have less. The Inuit from Igloolik have fifteen to twenty and sometimes twenty-five each for their long trip to Pond Inlet. If the snow is good, the huskies can travel fifty to seventy kilometres a day, and in extremely good conditions, they can cover one hundred or more kilometres.

The Arctic Vegetation

The vegetation in general is very poor consisting of moss, lichen and grass. Not a tree obstructs the view and shrubs will grow only a few centimetres from the ground. A large variety of flowers, often very small and delicate, taking advantage of the summer sun, adorn the tundra, giving it a joyful aspect that is underlined by the song of a multitude of migrating birds. Many different species arrive when the snow melts and are ready to leave at the first sign of frost.

Conclusion

The Catholic Mission of Pond Inlet is dedicated to the Sacred Heart of Jesus. Besides, it has the honour to own a relic of the Little Theresa, two small pieces of bone, and the

Huskies

Dog team

bell that is heard each day bears this inscription: "I am the bell of the great white silence. My name is Theresa of the Child Jesus. I was christened at the Carmel of Lisieux, May 17, 1930. Sister Agnes of Jesus, Saint Theresa's sister, was the first to make me sing the glory of God immediately after my baptism. Bishop Turquetil had me transported here in 1930."

The little steeple of the first Pond Inlet R.C. Mission

4

AMONG THE INUIT

The sound of the little bell reached Churchill calling Ataata Mari to Pond Inlet through the official obedience given by Bishop Lacroix. In August 1944, at Churchill, Father Rousselière boarded the *M. S. Nascopie*, the supply ship carrying a mixed cargo for the Hudson Bay trading posts. The boat stopped at Chesterfield Inlet from August 14 to 17, allowing him to meet at the Mission of Notre Dame de la Delivrande Fathers Arthur Thibert and Joseph Massé[1] and the Brothers Gilles-Marie Paradis[2] and Raymond Bedard[3] and also Father Marcel Rio[4] and Father Joseph Buliard who had arrived from Baker Lake by canoe, after a memorable trip that Father Rousselière illustrated in *Le Trait d'Union,* October 1945[5]. He was able to greet the

---

[1] Joseph Massé (1905-1975), Oblate missionary at Southampton, Repulse Bay and Chesterfield from 1931 to 1946 and then in the Indian missions of Manitoba.

[2] Gilles-Marie Paradis (1911-1984), Oblate Brother called "Ikkumaliriyi" by the Inuit of Chesterfield. He died in Churchill and is buried in the Churchill Cemetery.

[3] Raymond Bedard, born in 1909. Sent to Chesterfield Inlet from 1936 to 1957 as an Oblate Brother. He left the Oblates and worked for the Québec Government. Now deceased.

[4] Marcel Rio, French Oblate, (1899-1992). Cf. *Eskimo* N. S. N° 46, short biography by Charles Choque or the book by Hervé Aubin o.m.i. *Un vrai Inuk, Marcel Rio, Itinéraire d'un Homme de Foi.* (Novalis)

[5] *Le Trait d'Union* or *The Link*: the very first name of the *Eskimo* magazine.

These cartoons illustrate the trip by Fathers M. Rio and Buliard
from Baker Lake to Chesterfield, as observed by
Father G. M.-Rousselière, missionary at Pond Inlet

Mission Our Lady of the Delivrande—Chesterfield Inlet (c. 1944)

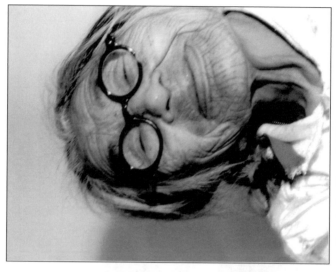

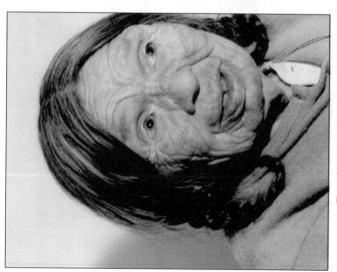

Two old Eskimo ladies Helene Kukilasak, Philomene Pangakrak—Chesterfield Inlet

devoted Grey Nuns who, since 1931, had taken care of the sick, the infirm and the elderly, and helped the mothers deliver their babies. On August 16, 1944, Father Rousselière had the joy of baptizing, using the Latin formula as was the custom then, Popopok, the daughter of Louis Suvisiq and Madeleine Mingiriak, born that morning. He named her Marie-Evangeline in honour of Sister Marie-Evangeline Gallant, the Superior General of the Grey Nuns of Nicolet who had just terminated her official visit of St.Theresa's Hospital. Marie Nanertak, the godmother, countersigned in syllabic characters the register of baptisms.

The *M. F. Therese*, in a dense fog, hit a reef not far from Salisbury Island, near Dorset, and sank, taking in the icy waters of the Hudson Strait all the provisions put on board for the missions, and even the personal effects of Bishop Lacroix, his pectoral cross and his mitre. Father Rousselière felt deeply such a loss affecting the entire Vicariate.

On August 17, the *Nascopie* left Chesterfield, made a short stop at Southampton Island, allowing Father Rousselière to visit St. Patrick's Mission where Father Rio was expected to take charge. Some Eskimos came to see him. They did not understand English and since Father Mary's knowledge of Inuktitut was practically non-existent, they could not communicate too well except by signs. On August 28th, the ice was so thick that the boat could not dock at Clyde River where two radio operators were supposed to leave the ship. Finally, on August 29, 1944, at 3:00 a.m., the *Nascopie* anchored at Pond Inlet. The noise of the chain, and the piercing cry of the siren, startled a multitude of seagulls and aroused from sleep the inhabitants of the village. Father Danielo hurried to greet Father Rousselière. Canon Turner, the Anglican minister, ran in great haste to welcome his fiancée,

Miss Joan Hobart. He asked Reverend Daulby to bless their union without delay in a ceremony held in the Saint Timothy Anglican Church. John Stanners went aboard to shake hands with Bert Swaffield, his replacement as manager of the Hudson Bay store. Louis Delisle went to meet Doug Webster and showed him the way to the R.C.M.P. detachment. Doug Webster was to replace him, keeping company to Michael Owens. Constable Owens had arrived a few days before on the *St Roch*, the R.C.M.P. boat commanded by the illustrious Inspector Henry Larsen. The *St Roch* had left Halifax on July 22 to sail through the difficult Northwest Passage, heading for Vancouver where it arrived on October 16th. This historical trip reaffirmed the sovereignty of Canada in the Arctic.

The next day, the Company's supply ship left on its way west, having as passenger Brother Carnevale[6] whose health was failing. It also carried for Arctic Bay 16 tons of coal extracted from the Pond Inlet mine. If not the best, it was at least the cheapest coal available. At the beginning of September, the weather remaining relatively mild, Fathers Danielo and Rousselière went to work at the mine, clearing the ground to uncover a portion of the coal vein to be exploited later. A goose, surely the last of the season, flew over them, just ahead of the first snow which developed into a violent storm that tore to pieces the tar paper covering the mission roof.

Already the small lakes were solidly frozen inviting people to come and fish through the ice. As soon as the snowstorm subsided Father Danielo went to try his luck. In three days, he caught five bags of fresh fish. Father Rousselière who had stayed home spent his time reading. He welcomed some visitors, among them, his confrère,

---

[6] Nazzareno Carnevale, Oblate Brother born in 1913 in Italy; stayed at Pond Inlet from 1942 to 1945. Left the Congregation, was married and resides in Toronto.

Reverend Daulby, of the Anglican Mission. Looking through the window not yet completely frosted, he could see the children and the ladies with babies on their back, laughing and shouting, running after the white ptarmigan landing in flocks around the post. On the still unfrozen portion of the sea, hunters in canoes, gun in hand and harpoons at the ready, were waiting for the seals to come up to the surface. In November, the trapping season opened; fox tracks were everywhere. With the temperature at 50° below zero, their fur would be thick and as white as snow.

One morning, Pannikpak, Qilirti's wife and her friend Ikirapik came to choose caribou skins to make a travelling outfit for Father Rousselière. They took his measurements without measuring tape, just looking at him. As they sewed, they told stories such as the following one copied by Father Danielo in the mission Codex, to the delight of Father Mary.

"Once upon a time, much before the arrival of the white man in the country, at Button Point, in an important Eskimo camp, an old Inuk wanted secretly to get rid of his son-in-law. Therefore, he asked him to come along hunting "akpas"—little murres—and help him to take eggs out of their nest. It was July. After walking a long time and crossing some mountains, they arrived at the summit of high cliffs where akpas by the hundreds had built their nests. The old man solidly attached an "*udjuk*" rope, a rope very strong made off the bearded seal's skin, around the body of his son-in-law and let him go down the flank of the cliff. The son-in-law, it is said, suspected foul play on the part of his father-in-law but nevertheless complied without a word. He had barely gone over the edge when the old man cried out that he could no longer hold his weight and that he was obliged to let the rope go free. The young man slid along the cliff but by an adroit manoeuvre succeeded in winding the rope around a sharp rock to stop his fall. A prisoner

Amaviapik (Pond Inlet)

Ikerapik, Eskimo lady—Pond Inlet

Okkomaluk

Inuit in a tent

between sky and water, he was able to reach a tiny platform from which he could neither ascend nor descend. The father-in-law had long left, convinced that his son-in-law was dead, crushed on the rocks below. But reality was something else! The tiny akpas were in large numbers. The son-in-law ate their flesh and stocked many birds for the days ahead. At first he suffered from thirst, but rain started to fall and he converted akpa skins into reservoirs of soft water. With skins also, he made some clothing and moccasins. Covered with feathers, he did not suffer too much from the cold. One day, the snow fell and slowly hardened in the cracks between the rocks. The young man was able to cut steps in the snow and to reach the top of the cliff, alive and full of joy. He was saved. It was dark when he arrived at the camp where everyone thought he was dead. The man who had replaced him as provider and husband, imagining he saw a ghost, took to his heels and disappeared. Crestfallen, the father-in-law huddled in a corner of the igloo, not daring to close his eyes all night long. The young man behaved naturally, as a hunter returning from the hunt, and no one dared to question him. He spent his time cutting and softening skin ropes, hour after hour, to a point that the father-in-law looking at him was obsessed by fear. One day, tired of observing his son-in-law cutting ropes, he fell asleep on his bed, his abdomen well exposed. The young man had been waiting all along for this moment. All his work with the ropes was indeed done to divert his father-in-law's attention. Seizing a large pointed icicle, he planted it in his belly and sent him to another world."

The winter of 1944-45 ended by a septic epidemic taking seven lives at Pond. When the disease hit the area, Reverend Turner and Daulby were absent, visiting Fort Ross and Clyde respectively. The Catholic mission and the R.C.M.P. took care of the sick and distributed sulpha drugs.

Hearing that Okkumaluk was very sick at Button Point, Father Rousselière asked Arnaviapik to take him to his camp. Arnaviapik agreed and Ataata Mari got acquainted with the use of a dog team and, more important, to the Inuit and their language. He gave some medicine to the sick and before leaving promised Okkumaluk he would return. Matter of fact, he went three times to the camps southeast of Bylot Island. Slowly, he was shaking off his natural shyness in front of the Native people. He confessed to Monseigneur Lacroix that sometimes he felt uneasy in the presence of a confrère and would prefer to remain silent. However, his relationship with his superior was excellent. Father Danielo had a gentle and quiet temperament. Both missionaries were happy to be among the Eskimos. Father Mary never asked to return to the Montagnais, notwithstanding the long polar nights which he never found as hard to bear as certain explorers. However, the lack of ministry lay heavy on his shoulders.

In May—the month he heard about the end of the Second World War—he kept the mission open during the absence of Father Danielo who had gone to Arctic Bay. He did the usual spring cleaning around the house. He wanted to decorate the chapel with a painting inspired by the North and personalized with local characters but, to do so, he needed Eskimo models and to get them, he photographed the most typical ones among the Mittimataligmiut, developing his own films, not without wasting many sheets of velox paper, as he admitted. He worked to install a rudimentary water main from a small lake above the house, an ingenious idea, which, according to him and following the law of gravity, would certainly be of great service during the summer.

In June, Father Rousselière accompanied Kublu's family as far as Bylot Island, hoping to be able to collect

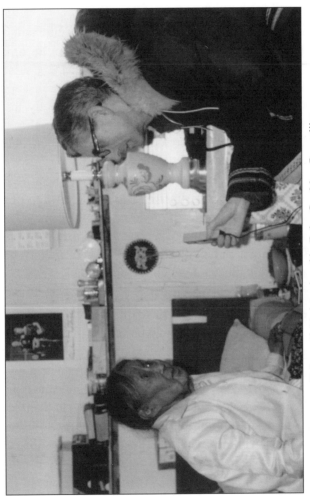

Rebecca Kublu interviewed by Father Guy Mary-Rousselière

some goose eggs, but four days later returned home with an empty bag. The season was late, the geese had not arrived. During the summer, he did a bit of gardening planting a few radishes, and some lettuce while his companion painted the exterior of the building.

In mid-July, the village was agog with excitement, the narwhals had appeared at the cracks that were becoming larger and larger in the sea ice. On August 25, a large bowhead whale emerged in front of the mission, just about 200 metres from the beach, attracting everybody there. Jumping in a canoe, Father Rousselière with the police and the HBC manager followed the whale for two hours before it disappeared. A few days later, on the *M. S. Nascopie*, Father Girard arrived and saw again the mission he had founded eleven years earlier. The Anglican Bishop of the Saskatchewan Diocese, Bishop Martin, was also aboard, and with three Oblates assisting, he blessed the marriage of Bert Swaffield, manager of the Hudson Bay Company. The ceremony took place on the boat.

The news of a tragedy that had occurred early in September at *Angmaraluit* in Milne Inlet reached Pond Inlet in October making an impact on the local population about the same as the second atomic bomb on Nagasaki did world wide. A small whale boat sailing along with a gentle breeze was overcome by a violent storm. It became rapidly filled with icy water and overturned plunging to their death three adults and four children. Kublu, Solange's husband, and Idlaut had left the whale boat earlier to follow the coast and pick up whale bones on the beach in order to use them later as runners for their sled. Never losing the boat from their sight, they had seen the drama. Wading through the water, they reached the capsized wreck and managed to bring to safety Solange and Thomas, the child she carried in her

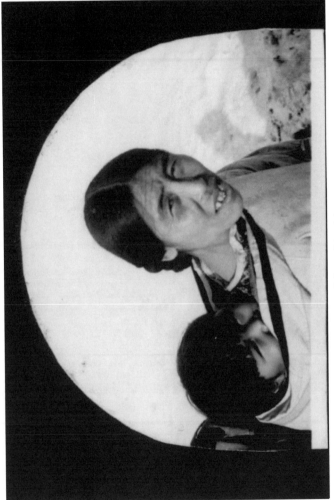

Solange Atagutsiar

Christmas 1945—Pond Inlet—the Chapel

hood. Half submerged, they had been holding on to the boat. Alas! Suzanne, Solange's little six year old girl, was dead.

Father Danielo went to Milne Inlet in November to console the parents of the victims. A difficult trip, and even a dangerous one, because of the bad snow and the fog that hid open water. Alone at home, Father Rouselière installed the electricity, hoping that the wind would activate the two windmills providing the current. In calm weather, during the long polar obscurity, or when a total eclipse happened, the Aladdin lamps were still coming to the rescue, supplying the light needed all day long.

Christmas 1945 was rather sad, not a single Catholic being present at the midnight service. The two Oblates celebrated Mass privately.The preceding Friday, a banquet had been given by the Honourable Company, with pudding and paper hats, a joyful event, but a poor compensation for the absence of priestly ministry. On Christmas day, in the evening, the Company organized a general dance. Father Rouselière paid a courtesy visit to the dancers and was very surprised to see the local beauties moving gracefully about in high heels!

On February 10, 1946, he baptized his first Tunnunirmiut, a small boy adopted by Kublu's family. Then, complying with a radio message from Bishop Lacroix, he prepared himself for a trip to Chesterfield Inlet, via Arctic Bay and Igloolik. Father Danielo had barely arrived from Clyde on February 18 when Ataata Mary left all wrapped up in his caribou outfit. Two days later, he was joined by the special constable of the Canadian Mounted Police, ordering him to turn about because a very contagious and fatal dog disease had broken out at Arctic Bay. He had no choice and returned to Pond Inlet where he spent March and April hunting seals and mining coal. It was only on May 5 that he resumed his trip to Arctic Bay where, two

Ittuliaq and Ivalaq, c. 1950

Arctic Bay

days before, Father Cochard had arrived from Igloolik. Ataata Mary had as guides Markusi Piungituk and Alain Maktar, two good companions, young but already full of experience and always willing to teach him Inuktitut. They followed the Navy Board Inlet and on the way visited many Inuit camps. The sea ice was far from being smooth, and filled with broken pieces of ice that bloodied the dogs' paws. Quite often, they had to travel by night, when the snow was hard and slippery. Of course, the word night was very relative at this time of the year, since daylight was nearly continual.

Here is how Father Mary-Rousselière described his arrival at Arctic Bay, May 16, 1946 at 7:00 a.m.: "We reached the end of Victor Bay from where a three mile portage separates us from the post. After an hour's climb, Arctic Bay is there before us, one of the most beautiful natural sights in the world. A steep descent of three quarters of a mile separates us from the post. We detach the dogs, a push on the sled and hope for the best! Very quickly, in spite of the ropes passed under the runners to act as breaks, the sled accelerates at great speed to stop only when reaching the shore of the bay. We hitch the dogs again to the sled and five minutes later we arrive at the post. The houses are built side by side on the flank of the hill. We first see the buildings of the Hudson Bay Company, then that of the Weather Station. Finally, at the very end, the little Mission with its neat little steeple...but no bell!"

Father Cochard, with the habitual exuberance of a happy Breton, welcomed him. They exchanged news concerning the Inuit, the Congregation and the Hudson Bay Vicariate that had just been divested of the missions situated along the Hudson Strait to form the new Apostolic Vicariate of Labrador entrusted to Monseigneur Lionel Scheffer. Together they paid a visit to Jimmy Bell, an extraordinarily stout Scotsman, manager of the Hudson Bay Company, to Hugh Longfield, officer in charge of the Weather Bureau, to Harold Serson, in charge of the Radio. They made the inventory of the supplies marked for the Mission of Igloolik, that had arrived by boat last summer. Father Rousselière baked bread and, according to Father Cochard, he made excellent bread. On a beautiful sunny day, he and Harold Serson climbed up Mount George V, whose summit reaches 600 metres above the sea. During the ascent, there was a minute of anxiety when, cutting steps in the hard snow, the Father lost his knife. From the peak, they enjoyed a superb view of the Bay, of Adams Sound and Strathcona Sound and even of the mountains boarding Admiralty Inlet on the west.

On Sunday May 26, Father Mary celebrated a High Mass for a few Catholics who had arrived from Igloolik. Later, after a festive meal, the men gathered together for a game of *nugluktartut*. Holes are drilled in a piece of bone a few centimetres long. The bone is then tied to a rope, made of caribou sinew, attached to the ceiling. A rotating movement is imparted to the rope and the winner is the one able to place his dart first in one of the holes. Of course, it is great fun.

Finally on May 28, with Pacôme Qulaut and Marc Idjangiark as guides, the two missionaries set out for Igloolik. They stopped at Moffet Inlet where Reverend Turner and his wife had settled, with June, their first child. At night, having put up the tent, they listened to the international news on the radio given to them by the Arctic Bay post. They arrived at *Ikpiarjuk* on June 8, just in time, the following day, to celebrate together with the impressive Igloolik Catholic community the feast of Pentecost: Kraingit, Anirniq Piuyuk! Come, Ô Holy Spirit!

Pacôme Qulaut

Igloolik

5

IGLOOLIK

The first Inuit conversions at Igloolik, go back to about 1930, thanks to the influence of Pierre Maktar, an Eskimo from Chesterfield Inlet who taught the elementary prayers and the Inuktitut hymns composed by Bishop Turquetil and the first missionaries.

It would be too long and outside our subject to give here the story of Father Bazin: his arrival at Igloolik, his settling at *Abvajar* Island in a shack made of old boxes and whose walls were covered with paper of all kind. A fire in July 1933, reduced to ashes his miserable shelter leaving him deprived of everything except a few calcinated dried beans. In the winter of 1934, Father Bazin went to Repulse Bay to visit Father Armand Clabaut[1] and Pierre Henry[2] and returned with his sled loaded with provisions but also unfortunately carrying back the dysentery bug which claimed victims among the people and the dogs. After spending the greater part of 1935 at Pond Inlet, Father Bazin returned to

---

[1] Armand Clabaut (1900-1966), Oblate Priest from Northern France; came to the Arctic in 1927. Elected Coadjutor to Bishop Turquetil in 1937, he returned to France in 1941.

[2] Pierre Henry (1904-1979), French Oblate from Brittany. In the Canadian North from 1932 to 1971, founder of the Pelly Bay, Spence Bay and Gjoa Haven Missions. Died at Sainte-Agathe-des-Monts. His biography *Kayualuk, Apostle of the Inuit* written by Charles Choque, o.m.i., is available at the Eskimo Museum, Box 10, Churchill, Manitoba, R0B 0E0.

Étienne Bazin, o.m.i.

Prayer book in syllabic script published in 1934

Abvajar in April 1936, where a small little cabin had been rebuilt. In 1937, as the Inuit settled at Igloolik, Father Bazin followed them and lived in an igloo erected by his parishioners. In February 1937, he received the visit of Reynold Bray and Graham Rowley[3], two explorers who had come by dog sled from Repulse Bay. Graham Rowley will later be among Father Mary-Rousselière's best friends, with a common denominator, a passion for archaeology.

After the first Synod of the Hudson Bay Vicariate held at Chesterfield in 1937, Monseigneur Turquetil's boat, the *M. F. Therese*, headed North and even reached Igloolik on September 14, with on board, Fathers Bazin and Jean-Marie Trébaol[4] who, once the unloading completed, began the construction of the very mission where Fathers Cochard and Mary-Rousselière arrived on June 8, 1946. At that time, the mission was a welcome halt for the travelling Inuit who would go in and out freely. Little by little, Father Rousselière settled down, made shelves, organized a dark room, photographed a small seal taken alive by François Tamnaruluk, later known as François Quassa. He developed the film and printed a few photographs. For him, taking photos was a hobby that would become little by little a fascinating art.

In September 1946, Father Mary-Rousselière wrote to Monseigneur Lacroix that he was studying the Eskimo archaeology with great interest. In fact, during the summer, he had spent a few days at *Pingerkalik*, said Mass there for the Inuit and had, with more or less accuracy, drawn a detailed plan of the Eskimo ruins, estimating that there were

---

[3] Cf. "*Cold Comfort: My Love Affair with the Arctic*" by Graham Rowley, page 85. McGill-Queen's University Press, 1996.

[4] Jean-Marie Trébaol (1905-1988), from Brittany. Missionary Oblate in Igloolik, Chesterfield, Cape Dorset, Repulse Bay, Whale Cove. Retired in 1969 to The Pas and in 1971, to France. He was a specialist in the genealogical trees of Inuit families.

Abvajar—Father Cochard

more than a hundred ancient habitations. Among these about twenty were of the "Tunit" type, rectangular in shape. He had also taken notes destined for the National Museum of Man in Ottawa, hoping that this would facilitate his acquisition of a license permitting him to continue his excavations. "The Queen, said Father Mary, is one of the most persistent diggers and spends most afternoons scratching the soil with a small knife!" The Eskimo woman, nicknamed *The Queen*, because of her respectable age and her influence in the camps, was in reality Monica Ataguttaaluk. Father Rousselière considered her as a living Eskimo encyclopedia who was willing to talk at anytime on the things of the past! In an article of the magazine *Inuktitut,* volume 66, Spring 1987, he acknowledged that he owed his love of Arctic archaeology to Monica Ataguttaaluk. In the *Eskimo*, vol. 37, September 1955, he had already written an article concerning her and entitled: *So Spoke the Queen of Igloolik.* It is my pleasure to reproduce here this article for the information of the readers:

"During the winter I spent at Abvajar near Igloolik, in 1947-48, my most constant visitor was old Monica Ataguttaaluk, better known as the "Queen of Igloolik". When I was not away travelling, hardly a day went by when I did not hear, coming from the porch, the characteristic slight cough which annouced the royal visitor.

To be frank, I would have much preferred these state visits to be either of shorter duration or longer spaced between. I even tried different ruses to avoid them. But it was a waste of time. Would I pretend to be asleep? Monica started coughing quietly, then gradually louder and louder and finished by clearing her throat with a loud gurgle. If that was not enough, with a voice like a top sergeant on the parade ground, she would ask: "Sinikpit? Are you asleep?" What normal sleeper could resist such treatment? If, on the contrary, I pretended to be doing some urgent work, she would come and look over my shoulder, starting the habitual litany of the sick children or the list of the expectant mothers with an indulgent "Keep on, you are not disturbing me"! I was no match for her!

I finally resigned myself to these daily visits, as one accepts a scourge of nature, and, imperceptibly, I came to enjoy them. Monica was a living Eskimo encyclopedia and God had given her the gift of a ready tongue. I therefore resolved to make her earn the ritualistic cup of tea which inevitably brought the royal audiences to a close by aiding me in revising an Eskimo vocabulary and giving me all sorts of information .

I can still picture her seated on the bench upon which her frequent visits had left a greasy patina, pulling from the top of her caribou socks the little bag which served her as a tobacco pouch and filing her pipe. She would then come and help herself to matches on the narrow shelf which served me as a combined desk and kitchen table. After a few puffs, she would start the story of her life:

"We did not always live on Abvajar Island, she said. We came to live here for the first time when my son Piwatu was in the "*amaut*"[5] (about 1905).

"We did not have real boats or "*umiaks*". Sometimes we used a sled covered with udjuk skins sewn together. For ferrying people and bagage, we also used two kayaks tied together. Crossing from Abvajar Island to the mainland was dangerous in those days as the walrus were so numerous.

"The kayaks were used mostly for hunting caribou, but also for chasing the walrus, a difficult and hazardous hunt as proved by the story of Mannerk whose craft was

---

[5] Amaut or pouch on the back of the woman's parka for carrying the baby.

overturned by a walrus he had harpooned. Mannerk fell in the water, came up again and clung to the tusks of the wounded beast but not for long. Going down again, he disappeared in the sea before help could reach him.

I had nine children in all. I would have had another baby but I lost it, I fell. When somebody was sick, we managed as best we could. We even performed operations. When my stepmother had a bad infection in one of her breasts, my father cut it off with a well sharpened knife and she recovered. We used to put seal blubber dressings on wounds to stop the bleeding and on abcesses, a fresh lemming skin.

"Do you know what a *qivittuk* is? That is a man who is mocked and who answers nothing, a scapegoat disgusted with life in general. I knew one in Pond Inlet; his name was Udlatitak. Everybody teased him and made fun of him, but he never said a word. One day, while I was visiting his wife, he took his rifle and put a bullet in his head. It was bound to happen; he was a *qivittuk*.

"The ptarmigans with their gizzards are funny birds; they eat only plants and berries and live just the same. They are very fat even in winter. They make little igloos in the snow to sleep in.

"The walrus also has a crop or rather two, one on each side of the neck, at the front. They fill them up with air and that is how they float and sleep on the surface of the water. They often sleep in pairs, side by side or back to back. They go mad like dogs and the males fight during the mating season. Some have been found with the tip of a tusk in their hide.

"What do the narwhals do with their tusks? I don't know but I saw one with a fish speared on his tusk. How did he manage to eat it, remains for me a mystery.

"The polar bears are good hunters. They even attack the walrus. My father saw a bear killing a walrus asleep on the ice. Hidden behind a hummock, the bear picked up a long piece of ice and went towards the walrus, walking on his hind feet and carrying the ice on his left shoulder. He felled the walrus with one blow of the ice. Though apparently dead, the tail of the walrus was still moving. The bear immediately started eating, pausing from time to time to lap up some snow. In another occasion, my father saw a bear pulling a walrus out of the water. Squatting on his behind, the bear was pulling with all the strength of his powerful jaws.

"The female polar bear spends part of the winter in a hole dug in the snow. It is there that the young are born. I knew an Eskimo who, unaware, walked over such a den and fell through the roof. He was so scared that he wet his pants. But the bear just sniffed and ran away without harming the poor fellow.

"A long time ago, I myself did kill a bear. We were at *Pingerkalik*. All the men were away hunting and we were just four women in the camp, Uttuit, Urulu, Kayak and myself. I was in my igloo with my little son Angiliq, about a year old, and young Kayak who was sleeping, when suddenly I heard pups barking and a big commotion in the snow porch. I stooped down to look out in the passage and there, before my eyes, were two huge paws and between, the bear's head! He was searching for food, snuffling and growling loudly; his nose wriggling like this... I hurriedly put Angiliq in my amaut, I woke up Kayak who immediately jumped into her boots and I armed myself with a knife. As I was smoking my pipe, I thought first I would blow smoke in the face of the bear to keep him from coming in. But I rather decided to take some pieces of seal blubber from the seal oil lamp and throw them to him.

When the bear was busy eating blubber, I hastily made a hole in the back of the igloo and jumped out with the baby. While Kayak ran to tell the neighbours, I grabbed a rifle leaning against a snowwall and a spear. Then I slid a bullet into the rifle and came back towards the igloo. The bear was just coming out of the porch and when he saw me, he started to run towards me, his head bent sideways, the way they do when ready to attack. I was shaking so much that I had to rest the rifle on the spear. The bear was roaring, his mouth wide open. I shot. The bullet entered the bear's mouth and he toppled over. I put another bullet into the rifle and shot again. The bear was dead. In the meantime, my baby had fun, poking his head over my shoulder and looking at what was going on!

The bear was already skinned and cut up when the hunters returned. They had killed nothing. When my husband heard what had happened, he burst out laughing because the women had killed a bear while the men had returned empty-handed. In fact, it was very funny!

Monica told me many other stories which unfortunately I did not record. She was to die the following summer. More than once, I was tempted to ask her about the circumstances in which, forty-five years before, she had eaten her first husband and children, but something held me back. Had she known, she would probably have laughed at my scruples."

Father Guy Mary-Rousselière's vocation as archaeologist was going back further than *Pingerkalik*. In France during his studies, he was influenced by Father Roger Chrétien, an Oratorian priest, holder of a diploma in Natural Sciences, Professor at the St Martin School of Pontoise. He was also influenced by the Reverend Henri Breuil, (1877-1961), Professor at the College of France, a renowned historian who shared the infatuation of the

French clergy of that time for the palaeolithic discoveries and rupestrian paintings and with whom he will keep in touch.

In all simplicity, he admitted seeing no conflict of interest in being a missionary and an archaeologist: "There is no contradiction, he wrote, between the study of God, Theology, and the study of Man, God's creature. At all events, certain discoveries could lead to a better knowledge of the ancestral religious practices of the Inuit". He never neglected his ministry because of his hobby. He heard confessions, gave, in Inuktitut, little sermons duly corrected by Father Didier. The latter had arrived from Repulse in mid-September on the Peterhead of Donat Anaruar with James Nilaulak, Robert Tati and René Inusituarjuk as the crew. He replaced Father Cochard who had been called to Rome to participate in the Oblate General Chapter. In winter Father Rousselière set a few traps and, December 3, caught his tenth fox, his humble contribution to the payment of the new Vicariate boat, the *Regina Polaris.*

The *Regina Polaris*—the mission boat

Théophile Didier, o.m.i.

In January 1947, dressed like an Eskimo in caribou skins, in 45° below zero weather, he left for a three week trip to Baffin Land and Jens Munk Island to visit several Inuit camps. He arrived at *Siurarjuk* in a blizzard strong enough to break the tusks of a walrus, he would note in the Codex. Later, at *Tassiuyark*, he baptized the infant Robert Kattarainuk, born the night before to Madeleine Tulugardjuk. Then he headed towards *Kapuivik*, a camp with seven igloos. Sitting on the sled he tried to protect himself from the cold. The dogs were running at a good pace and he was tossed about to the rhythm of the snow drifts. Unseen by him, the *kudliq, or seal oil lamp,* fell off the sled as well as several packages of tobacco. Father Didier writing of this incident in the Codex assumed that Ataata Mary was in the clouds! The two Oblates very rarely missed an occasion to tease each other. Father Rousselière's long ride had not been a pleasure trip. The blizzard had slowed him down, he had been short of food; so much so that, when he returned to the mission on January 29, he could sincerely say: "Our Father, give us this day our daily nourishment", according to the new formula accepted by the Church at the demand of the missionaries of the Canadian North, certainly a more appropriate formula since the Inuit did not eat bread.

On April 1, Father Danielo arrived bringing with him from Pond Inlet many letters addressed to Father Rousselière; the news, dating from the preceding summer, was not very fresh but welcome anyway. On the 5th of April, Holy Saturday, Kayukuluk,—Father Danielo's Inuktitut name—baptized Pacôme and Alain's little girls, Christina and Josée-Marie. Both died of the flu within a few days. At Easter, about one hundred Inuit participated in the liturgy and enjoyed various games. The children had fun wearing masks fabricated by Father Rousselière.

Children of Igloolik with masks made by Guy Mary-Rousselière at Easter

On April 17, Father Rousselière and his guide Bernard Ikkuma left for Arctic Bay to recover the supplies unloaded last year from the *Nascopie* and marked for the R.C. Mission of Igloolik. During his absence, Mitch Owens, the R.C.M.P. Constable of Pond Inlet arrived by sled in Igloolik. He was issuing the Inuit identification disks bearing a district number. He also took the census of the population in order to facilitate a fair distribution of the family allowances. On May 1, he returned to Pond Inlet. On the 5th, Father Danielo followed him but went through Arctic Bay to meet Father Rousselière who had arrived there on April 31st.

In Arctic Bay, they heard a fantastic story concerning the end of the world publicized by a lady called Ikkuma. Ikkuma, Alluluk's wife, died, went to heaven and came back to earth to announce the apocalypse. She even threatened to shoot two people who did not believe her. Her mandate was to go to all the camps in the vicinity of Arctic Bay and deliver her message that the end of the world was near. Consequently, men and women had to abandon themselves to a total sexual licentiousness. Fortunately, Canon Turner got wind of Ikkuma's wild imaginings and, with the collaboration of the police, was able to put an end to this new pseudo-religious theory.

Father Rousselière returned to Igloolik only on June 16, meeting many Inuit on the way and crossing the trail of Reverend Turner. The going was slow because of the intense cold, the wind and the blowing snow that obliged them to put up camp early. Arriving home, he found Father Didier sowing lettuce, a whole package of seeds in a tiny box, he noted with humour in the mission Journal.

Ataata Mary was adapting himself more and more to the Inuit customs. At the end of June, he left with them to pick up around *Nirlirnartok*, duck and goose eggs but without much success. On August 7, 1947, he accompanied the Inuit in their hunt for walruses, seals, and white whales and he came back with a good stock of photos and archaeological notes concerning the surrounding of *Alarnerk*.

On September 11, the mission boat, the *Regina Polaris*, dropped anchor in the bay of Igloolik. Bishop Lacroix was on board and gave Father Didier an obedience for Repulse Bay, to be replaced at Igloolik by Father Bazin. At the beginning of October, bad news was broadcasted on the C.B.C. Radio. At Moffet Inlet, Canon Turner was fatally wounded.This tragic event which happened on September 24, 1947 is described in Reverend John Hudspith Turner's biography, written in 1949 by Maurice S. Flint, himself an Arctic Missionary from 1936 to 1941. The book *Turner of the Arctic* is illustrated with beautiful photographs and is dedicated to June, Grace and Faith the three daughters of Canon Turner and to his wife Joan Miriam Hobart. The Anglican priest was returning home after a short incursion on the sea in pursuit of a seal. Holding his rifle under the arm, he wanted to help a young Inuk girl to carry a pail of ice. When going up the stairs to his home, the rifle slipped and fired, wounding him mortally in the face and brain. On November 21, he was evacuated by a DC3 of the Canadian Aviation, named *The Blizzard Belle*, that had been delayed by the bad weather and the polar night,... but it was too late. On December 9, he died at the General Hospital in Winnipeg.

At Igloolik the two missionaries lived in the vacant house of the Hudson Bay Company which, temporarily, had closed its doors. So it became their task to distribute the family allowances, milk, pablum, rope for nets, caribou skins to make clothing and other usual products. There were then about 160 children who were receiving five dollars each month. Often Father Rousselière harnessed the dogs and travelled to *Abvajar* to pick up things left behind in the mission or to visit some Inuit in order to baptize a newborn child or take care of a broken leg. At Christmas, about a hundred persons swarmed into the mission to pray and to rejoice.

In March 1948, Father made a short exploratory trip into Baffin Land and, on April 1, he left for Pond Inlet with William Okkumaluk. As a result, he was not at Igloolik to welcome *Arctic Wings* when the plane arrived from Churchill on April 5. On board were Father Ferron, Brother Bedard and Dr. Joseph Moody, the medical doctor in charge of the Chesterfield Hospital. The plane left the next day taking away Father Bazin whose health was a bit shattered. Brother Bedard remained at Igloolik to help with the transformation of the mission.

As usual after the departure of a boat or a plane, a flu epidemic broke out causing the death of several Natives. Father Rousselière did not return to Igloolik until June 5, too late to assist the dying. He brought back with him on the sled, Alex Elder's tombstone. Allow me to copy out here the notes given by Father Rousselière himself. We will certainly notice the precision of all the details.

"The winter 1947-1948 marked the 125th anniversary of Parry's stay in Igloolik. The expedition under his command had left England on the 8th of May 1821, aboard His Majesty ships Fury and Hecla. Parry had received instructions from the Admiralty to follow the northern coast of the North American continent in order to discover the hypothetical North-West Passage. The two ships hibernated at Winter Island, south east of Melville Peninsula. They got caught in the ice and only after 267 days were they able to resume their search in a northern direction. They were unable, because of the ice, to enter into the Gulf of Boothia and again Parry had to resign himself to spend another winter in a bay of the Igloolik Island, not very far from the actual site of the R.C.Mission and HBC store.

That is the very spot where, on April 15th 1823, was going to die Alexander Elder. Captain Lyon, the ship's captain, wrote about this sad event in his private diary:

"On April the 15th, Mr. Alexander Elder, Greenland Mate of the Hecla, departed this life, after a confinement of a few days. His complaint was a confirmed dropsy, which had considerably swelled his whole body and limbs, and the poor man suffered continued and severe pain from the oppression in his chest, which, on examination after death, was found to contain six pints of water. During both winters, he had been subject to disorders in the breast and side, and for some time past, had been in a great measure under the eye of the surgeon. The deceased had been a leading man with Captain Parry on Captain Ross' voyage, and for his good conduct had been made mate of the Griper on the last expedition. Now having overcome the second winter of a third voyage, the poor fellow was fated to breathe his last at Igloolik. He was a thorough and steady seaman, and solely by his own merit had risen to the station which he filled at the time of his death.

"During the 16th, a party were employed digging a grave, but after many hours of labour, and breaking ten pick axes, were unable, on account of the frozen state of the earth, to penetrate deeper than three feet.

"On the forenoon of the 17th, the officers and crews of both ships attended the remains of their deceased comrade to the grave, and, the Rev. Mr. Fisher being confined by illness, Captain Parry, as senior officer and patron of the defunct, read the funeral service. Two volleys were fired over the grave, and we returned on board amidst the clouds of snow, which were flying under the influence of the most severe northerly gale we had experienced during the winter."

The grave of the unfortunate sailor was left unattended for many years. When the Catholic Mission was established in Igloolik in 1933, all traces of the tomb had disappeared.

According to what old Inuit have told, many years ago, some Eskimos decided to open the tomb, hoping to find some useful objects. All they discovered was a wooden coffin containing the remains of Alexander Elder. They took the wood and abandoned on the spot all the bones. As for the tombstone, it is only thirty years ago that it received some attention. An Eskimo brought it on his sled to Albert Harbour, at the entrance of Pond Inlet, where there was a trading post. The tombstone was installed in the little graveyard where until recently it was possible to see it together with two other tombs of sailors. I took it from there last spring to bring it back to Igloolik. The tombstone measures about two feet by one and is made of a slate of limestone quite hard as the one found profusely on Igloolik Island. Crudely cut and rounded on the top, it was remarkably polished on the face where this inscription has been engraved with great care:

Mr.ALEX^R ELDER
GREEN^D MATE
H.B.M. SHIP HECLA
OBt. APRIL 15th 1823
AGED 36 YEARS

Last summer, from Igloolik, we went to look for the exact location of the grave. An old Eskimo gave us so many clues that in no time we found it on a spit of land on the east coast of Thurton Bay, approximately two miles from the

To the memory of Alex Elder (1823)

village. It was situated on a very low embankment, about three hundred metres from the shore, probably the first spot free of snow discovered by the sailors of the Hecla.

Within a radius of two or three hundred metres, we found human bones and two skulls. One of the dolichocephalic type seems quite old and could very well be the skull of Alexander Elder. The other one of brachycephalic type was more recent. Among the bones collected, there was also a long femur. Incidentally, the tomb's measurements are such, according to the Inuit, that the deceased must have been a man of great stature.

On the 10th of August, a cairn was erected alongside the old grave surmounted by a long white stone so as to be more visible against the dark background. At its base, were buried all the human bones found in the vicinity. The tombstone proper is embedded halfway up the tumulus, practically at the very location where the courageous pioneer was buried, facing the anchorage of the Hecla, 125 years ago.

On July 16th, 1948, in the morning, while Father Rousselière was visiting the Inuit at the camp of *Kangik*, the Queen of Igloolik died peacefully. She had never really recovered from a bout of spring influenza. She was well prepared having received the sacrament of the sick a few days earlier. She was buried immediately as the Inuit were anxious to depart for their seasonal walrus hunt. Ataata Mary accompanied them hoping they would return on Saturday night in order to be able to assure the Sunday Mass. They got lost in the fog and it was only on Monday that they came back after spending the day of the Lord on the water.

Father Rousselière was invited to Chesterfield Inlet for two good reasons: first, to enjoy the retreat preached by Father Paul Dumouchel, the future Bishop of the

Keewatin and secondly, to greet, on July 29, the Very Reverend Leo Deschâtelets, the Superior General of the Congregation. Travelling conditions did not permit him to leave Igloolik.

On August 20, the *Notre-Dame,* the Peterhead of the Chesterfield mission arrived with Fathers Cochard, Danielo and Antonio Ostan[6] on board. James Nilaulak and Paul Kunuk who accompanied them had killed two bears on the moving ice near Cape Wilson. On the 28th, the small boat, not bigger than a nut shell dancing on the waves, set off again for Repulse Bay with Father Mary-Rousselière and Brother Bedard on board. They arrived in *Nauya,* August 31st, a few hours before the *Regina Polaris* which had as passengers Bishop Lacroix, Father Vandevelde[7] and Brother Paradis. The unloading of the *Polaris* began immediately in spite of the wind and the rain, in order to allow the ship to go off to sea early the next day. On land, there was no lack of work for the Oblate visitors. They helped with the construction of a shed to store the annual supplies. On September 13, Father Rousselière embarked on the *Severn,* the HBC boat, and arrived at Chesterfield Inlet three days later during a big storm!

---

[6] Antonio Ostan, Italian Oblate born in 1920. After several years in the North, his health forced him to come South. He is presently ministering to the Korean population of Ottawa.

[7] Frans Vandevelde, Belgian Oblate born in 1909. He came to the Arctic in 1937, spending most of his missionary life in Pelly Bay and Hall Beach (Sannerajak). In 1986, he left the North and retired in his home country.

Paul Kunuk, Madeleine Tulugarjuk and family

6

BAKER LAKE

The St. Paul Mission of Baker Lake, *Qamanittuaq* in Inuktitut,—a word which means a lake crossed by a river, in this case the Thelon River—goes back to 1927, built on the west bank of the lake with wood initially bought to build the Pond Inlet Mission. Because of a change in the schedule of the *Nascopie,* the building material was unloaded at Chesterfield Inlet and later transported to Baker Lake by a Company schooner. This boat, badly damaged by the ice and taking in water like a sponge, left Chesterfield on September 12, 1927 with Bishop Turquetil, Father Rio and Father Clabaut on board. The trip was unforgettable! Fog, wind, reefs, shipwreck, in a word anything hell could imagine to stop the construction of a new mission for the Kairnirmiut of Baker Lake. But fortunately, Little Theresa intervened and on the 18th, the schooner anchored at the west end of the lake. The wood, the flour, the beans, the rice, everything was soaked. The only things the Oblates had left were their enthusiasm, a barrel of nails, a hammer and their inexperience as carpenters! When eight days later, Bishop Turquetil went back to Chesterfield in the R.C.M.P. large canoe, the main part of the construction was up in spite of the blowing snow that had forced the improvised carpenters to work fully dressed in caribou clothing and with mittens. Three years later, Father Rio bought some

Saint Paul Mission—Baker Lake

abandoned buildings from the Dominion Explorers, moved them to the north shore of the lake, approximately where the new mission built in 1957 stands today.

The Oblates arrived in Baker not long after the Reverend Smith, the Anglican Minister who had already succeeded in drawing to him most of the Native people, warning them against the men in black robes. Only a few poor families living around the Kazan had not been influenced by either denomination. Joining their small number to the Inuit living at the entrance of lake Baker, they formed the humble nucleus of the local Catholic congregation.

On September 24, 1948, Father Mary-Rousselière arrived at Baker Lake on board the *Earl Trader*. He was to replace the younger Father Choque, Charles, who was sent to Chesterfield Inlet. Joseph, Charles' brother, ten years older, had succeeded Father Rio in 1944. He gave Father Rousselière a warm welcome.

Alas! Father Guy arrived too late to meet his friend Joseph Buliard who had returned to Garry Lake a few days earlier with most of his annual supplies. There was no hope of visiting him either, for the plane, a *Norseman*, which had flown to Garry Lake, on its return to Baker Lake was completely put out of commission by a violent gale which threw the aircraft against some heavy boards recently unloaded and piled up on the beach. A real loss, but luckily without human casualty. Charley Weber, the co-pilot, stayed at the mission awaiting a chance to go back to Churchill. To kill the time, he went ptarmigan hunting with the priests, happy to contribute to a more varied menu on the mission's table.

Around the end of October, Father Rousselière helped to set a few nets under the ice, hoping to take enough fish

Joseph and Charles Choque, o.m.i.—Baker Lake 1947

Joseph Buliard checking his fish nets

Inuk showing his son how to set a fox trap

to feed the dogs during the winter. Not an easy task for the ice surface was rough having been broken many times by the wind. The fishing turned out to be poor, only 25 fish in six days for four nets.

Early December, he left by dog sled to visit old Nutarartar who had been sick all summer. Nutarartar was living in a small dirty igloo not far from the Kazan River. The state of his health did not inspire confidence, so much so that Father Rousselière gave him the sacrament of the sick, making on his forehead the Sign of the Cross with some oil specially blessed. On his return, six days later, the thermometer was recording 45° below zero.

The cold however did not discourage the Inuit who arrived in great numbers to celebrate Christmas at the settlement.Twenty-nine Catholics, Sarvarturmiut from around the Kazan River and Ukkusiksaligmiut from Garry Lake, attended the Midnight Mass. The following days, they traded their family allowances and the few white foxes they caught in their traps. It was not a good year for trapping. The fur cycle was at its lowest. The year ended in a frightful blizzard.

First Return to France

Having received permission from Bishop Lacroix to visit his family in France, Father Mary first thought of going to Churchill by dog team via Padlei and Duck Lake. The bad weather made him change his mind and on January 26, 1949, he landed in Churchill on a DC3 plane that had brought into Baker provisions and mail for the D.O.T. or Department of Transport and for the army personnel based there since the *Musk Ox* expedition of 1947.

On February 26, 1949, Father Mary-Rousselière boarded the *Queen Mary* bound for France. World War II had given him many anxieties concerning his relatives but today, he was happy to be with them and to be introduced to four new young nieces. He relaxed reading "Tintin" and also spent a short stay in the hospital for a hemorrhoidal operation. He brought a small collection of Eskimo antiquities found in Igloolik to the Museum of Man in Paris and with the second in command, he discussed the possibility of an expedition in the North that he would evidently be asked to accompany. He immediately submitted the project to his Bishop, telling him that the Superior General encouraged him strongly to study anything related to Eskimo anthropology. During his holidays, he also gave lectures in Paris and in the suburbs where the Oblates were not well known. He also spoke to the scholastics of Solignac, rekindling in many of them their ardour for the northern missions. After six months with his family, he embarked on the *M.S. Caronia* on August 23 to return to Canada.

Once in Churchill, during the fall, he visited the Indians at Duck Lake, travelling aboard the Canso plane bringing supplies to the H.B.C. trading post. He found about 120 Indians, 32 of whom were Catholics. The mission without a resident priest was in a pitiful state. The Montagnais, themselves, were not aware of the tragedies in store for them as a result of a relocation to Churchill in 1956. The idea of the Agent to move them to Churchill did not please them. Presently, generally speaking, Catholics as well as Protestants really feel bitter, having the impression that no one cared for them. Father Egenolf had been on his way the previous winter to visit them but half-way on the trip, he became ill and had to turn back. Father Rousselière reported the sad situation existing at Duck Lake to the Fathers at Reindeer Lake hoping they could in some way solve the problem.

At the Bishop's house in Churchill, he prolonged his visit to help Father Jean Philippe[1] prepare the next two issues of *Eskimo*. In the December 1949 issue, he published an article on Father Prime Girard, *"The Pastor of the North Pole"*, who had died on July 30 of the same year. In the March 1950 issue, he described with humour and sympathy the rich personality of Monica Ataguttaaluk mentioned previously in the book. He revealed in these articles his talent as a writer: great precision, pleasant style, sound ideas and furthermore, on the cover of the magazine, he showed without the slightest shadow of a doubt his artistic talent, drawing for us the portrait of the late Pilagapsi, with his long hair as was the style earlier, and the face of a beautiful Eskimo woman of Igloolik in her traditional costume. He did not hesitate to tell Monseigneur Lacroix that he had no real attraction for Churchill and that he was planning to take the first plane available to return to Baker Lake.

On October 30, 1949, Father Henri-Paul Dionne[2] of Eskimo Point Mission, now Arviat, disappeared in the waters of Hudson Bay with two Inuit. He was transporting by canoe to the Maguse River heavy batteries used to provide electric lighting. To this day, the cause of the tragedy remains unknown. Late in autumn, meteorological conditions are not ideal: storms are sudden and violent, ice is beginning to form, visibility is sometimes nil and in the shallow bays, the rocks are level with the water ready to smash the bottom of any boat foolhardy enough to take the risk. At the invitation of Father Ferron, Bishop Lacroix's

---

[1] Jean-Claude Philippe, o.m.i., born in France in 1909, missionary in Arviat, Qamanittuaq, Salliq and Churchill. Co-founder of the *Eskimo* magazine. A former army chaplain, he is now retired in Thunder Bay, Ontario.

[2] Henri-Paul Dionne (1905-1949), French Canadian Oblate; went up North to Salliq in 1932 and in 1935 to Arviat. Cf. his biography *J'étais Routier en Terre Stérile* par Eugène Nadeau, o.m.i., (Montréal, Les Études Oblates 1951).

Pilagapsi (drawing by Father Guy Mary-Rousselière)

right hand man at Churchill, Father Rousselière went immediately to Arviat to take over the St.Therese mission left vacant and in disarray by Father Dionne's death. Father François Bérubé[3] was then at Padlei and having heard of the tragedy by the R.C.M.P., he hurried back to Eskimo Point. Monseigneur Lacroix was in Rome. Before leaving for the Eternal City, he had given Father Bérubé permission to visit his relatives in the province of Quebec during the winter, even if he had to close the mission of Padlei. Without a clear order from his Superiors, Father Rousselière felt a bit ill at ease to take the direction of the Arviat mission. Moreover, because of his natural timidity, and knowing neither the country nor the Inuit, nor their dialect, he considered himself the least capable of assuming such a responsibility among the Padlermiut. Another good reason for not staying in Arviat was that, according to their customs, the inland Eskimos would not come to the Post before spring. Moreover, Father Joseph Choque was expecting him in Baker Lake, anxious to take holidays with his family in Belgium.

After picking up his luggage in Churchill, Father Rousselière boarded the first plane of the year 1950, and flew to Baker Lake on January the 11th. The cold although biting was bearable due to the complete absence of wind. At the beginning of March, Father Choque left Baker Lake and Father Rousselière stayed alone until August when Father Georges Lorson[4] arrived from France. The Codex of the Saint Paul Mission described the daily occupations of the two missionaries who had to hunt or fish in order to provide daily dog food, who had to welcome the Inuit,

[3] François Bérubé (1917-1982), French Canadian Oblate; in the North from 1943 to 1954.

[4] Georges Lorson, French Oblate, born in 1923. After a short stay in Sri Lanka, he came to the Hudson Bay Diocese in 1950. He has served in several missions and is presently in charge of the Rankin Inlet R.C. Parish.

Paul Arnajuinnar—Baker Lake

Guy Mary-Rousselière visiting a fish net

listening to them telling their precarious or hopeless situations, to undertake emergency trips to the camps touched by famine, to visit the sick, to attend and evacuate a woman who attempted suicide and to mend all kinds of matrimonial troubles! All that without mentioning some mild altercations with the Police, some strained relationships with the Anglican Minister concerning mixed marriages and a thousand and one other things that kept them on the alert. The mission was also a natural haven for many of the official visitors coming by plane or by boat, even cameramen from the National Film Board or employees of the Department of Transport.

But the sky was not always grey. From time to time, a ray of sunshine was bringing joy to their souls. For instance, the baptism of Kanayuk, Paul Arnajuinnar's wife, an excellent soapstone sculptress to whom Father Mary gave his own mother's name, Yvonne; or the arrival of Father Buliard, the hermit of Garry Lake, who was completing a long trip that took him first to the mouth of the Back River and Sherman Inlet. He had Joanny Makidgak as his guide. April the 25th, 1950, was the precise date of his arrival. I know, since I was myself a visitor in Baker Lake at the time, having arrived that same day at 1:00 a.m. from Chesterfield Inlet with Victor Sammurtuk as my guide and Constable Martin Donnan and Norman Ford as our travel companions.

In May 1950, in order to visit the people of the Kazan, Father Rousselière left the teaching of the children to the care of Father Buliard. Accompanied by René Naituk, he departed for the camps of Marc Samgusak, George Tataniq, Timothy Kiorut and Nicolas Niurtuk. After a miserable winter, the caribou had finally reappeared, thus ending a period of famine that only a few fish caught from under the ice had barely allowed to overcome. Father's return to the

Timothy Kiorut and his son (on the Kazan River at Baker Lake)

settlement coincided, within one hour or two, with the furious blizzard which on May 19 broke the propeller of the windcharger and piled the snow as high as the roof on the houses, obliterating all the windows.

Naituk's joy was great when, in June, he saw a few caribou on the hill behind the settlement. He killed one caribou which was soon entirely devoured by the dogs. Immediately, informed that Naituk had killed a caribou, the policeman, Bill Ripley, had sent his special constable Uyumrak to warn him that he had acted illegally because the hunting season was closed. Naituk did not believe that, as an Inuk, he could not provide meat for his family. He asked Father Rousselière to accompany him to the Police Detachment as interpreter. This is approximately the dialogue that ensued.

Naituk: "Who denounced me?" Bill evidently did not compromise himself and refused to tell him the name of his informer, adding that Whites and Eskimos living in the village must all abstain from hunting the caribou during the closed season.

Naituk: "Why don't you visit my tent? You would then see that there is nothing to eat". Bill answered him that if he was not so lazy, he would go fishing.

Naituk: "Fishing is no good. With five nets, your employees took two fish in two days!" Bill replied that at this time of the year, angling for trout is more profitable.

Naituk: "I already went line fishing and I took nothing." Breathless with impatience, Bill reaffirmed simply the law that forbids the killing of caribou during the closed season.

Naituk: "Why then did the Company clerk recently kill two pregnant females?" With this, the policeman no longer able to argue, simply threatened to put Naituk in jail if he did commit a second offence. Naituk answered that after all

114

he had not known that killing caribou was forbidden and he promised that he would not do it again. And, probably switching to another ground, he added, it's the same for the geese! Bill didn't understand him and had the feeling that Naituk was calling him names. "No, said Father Rousselière who had so far been silent, he is not calling you names, he is just saying something about geese!" Then the outraged policeman sent Uyumrak to seize Naituk's rifle and bullets. Father Rousselière then, sensing that the situation could turn out to be tragic for Naituk's family, intervened: "So you would not even give him permission to kill a few caribou?" "Let him come Monday morning to ask my authorization", answered the Constable. "He is one of the less resourceful Eskimos that I know. After all, why didn't he return to Chesterfield this spring?" "With only three poor dogs", answered Father, "he was really unable to make such a trip". "And why not", replied the policeman, "others have done it in worse conditions".There was nothing to add and thus ended the interview. The Canadian "Mounted" Police representative had once again mounted his high horse but luckily in the fresh fallen snow, all tracks quickly vanish.

Early in July, the tundra came alive again with birds and insects. Father Rousselière, brandishing an appropriate net, could be seen running in pursuit of butterflies to help a university entomologist to increase his collection and to study the twelve or more species living in the Arctic. The ice started to move on the lake, allowing amphibious planes to land on the water and boats to announce their arrival. In August, the whole village rejoiced at the coming of the *Regina Polaris* soon followed by the *Severn* which anchored at a short distance from the shore. The three missionaries, Rousselière, Buliard, and Lorson put on their working overalls and brought the mission's supplies from the shore to the warehouse. They also transported out of reach of the waves a few dozen bags of coal whose dust blackened their faces. Absorbed in their work, they were unaware of what was going on at the other end of the settlement where Reverend James was proceeding in all solemnity and tranquillity to the marriage of the Inuk known as the "Limper", an Anglican, with a slightly hysterical Catholic girl. In presence of a fait accompli, it was too late for the R.C. priests to raise their arms to heaven. The woman's father and the bride pleaded ignorance; they did not know, so they pretended, a bit shamefully, that the marriage could not be valid in the eyes of the Catholic Church if performed by the "*Ajukirtuyi*". *Ajukirtuyi* is the inuktitut word for "Minister" and means the one who teaches. Reverend James knew the disappointment of his papist colleagues and sent them a few leaves of green lettuce, probably a bit bitter to the taste, but a graceful gesture anyway, since fresh vegetables were so rare in the North.

On August 23, Father Buliard went back to Garry Lake aboard *Arctic Wings*. The small plane was heavily loaded and had a canoe tied to one of its pontoons. The Norseman flew over the Aberdeen region where the kingdom of the muskox began. Five days later, Doug Wilkinson and Jean Roy of the National Film Board, passing through Baker Lake, were able to photograph about thirty muskoxen in the Thelon Sanctuary. As for Father Rousselière, walking in the tundra, he simply had to content himself with catching live *siksiks*, a species of ground squirrels living in burrows under small hillocks usually covered with grass. He had to send his catch to the "Nordic Research Laboratories of the Defence Department". It was almost a fruitless hunt; of the three specimens he captured, two escaped "lui brûlant la politesse". He was luckier hunting ptarmigans and came home with 32 birds which had so far avoided the hungry foxes whose tracks were everywhere.

A strange phenomenon, on September 23, obscurity covered Baker Lake. The forest fires burning out of control in Saskatchewan and Manitoba, fanned by the wind, released such dense smoke that it completely hid the sun, creating an apocalyptic scene.

In October, as usual, it was back to fishing under the ice. No caribou were reported on the tundra around Baker Lake and some unlucky Inuit had already lost a few dogs from starvation. Garry Lake, on the contrary, had enjoyed such an abundance of caribou during the summer that Father Buliard was able to travel to the camps and live among the catechumens he had to prepare for baptism without fear of being short of food. In a letter delivered by Pie Korsut arriving November 26 at Baker Lake and addressed to Father Rousselière, Father Buliard stated that he was on his way to Perry River. Everyone knew Perry River, the small kingdom of Angulalik, an Inuk, holder of the Coronation medal, manager of the Hudson Bay Store, a man with such a strong personality and a temperament so irascible that he would plunge, it is said, his dagger in the belly of any Inuk reckless enough to oppose him.

The beginning of the year 1951 was disastrous for the Inuit at Baker Lake. They arrived at the post in rags, walking and helping two or three scrawny dogs to pull the sled. They would not have survived without the help they received from different local institutions. The Trading Company with her moto: *"Pro Pelle, Cutem",* had no interest in letting the Inuit hunters and trappers, die of hunger.The Mounted Police was conscious of its duty to look after the welfare of the Natives. The Radio and Meteorological Stations were not directly involved but preferred to give their surplus to the poor Inuit rather than throwing it in the garbage. The Missions, well aware of the evangelical value of sharing, could not close their eyes on the misery of the local population. However, they also remembered the proverb "God helps those who help themselves", encouraging the Inuit to look for their daily food; too often, one could see that certain individuals were too traumatised to search for game.

In reference to the tragic situation of January 1951, here is what Father Rousselière wrote:

"I shall never forget the January day at Baker Lake when an Eskimo named Marc Samgusak staggered into the post on foot. His dogs, he told us, had long since starved. Now his family was dying of hunger, some 40 miles to the south. The herds of caribou upon which he and other inland Eskimos depended had not followed their usual migration route. Famine shadowed the land.

"We loaded my sled with supplies and left at dawn. At dusk on the second day, we spied a tiny white dome nearly lost amid distant snowdrifts. Marc, who had frozen both heels the night before, jumped clumsily from the sled and hobbled forward. Ignoring the drifted snow at the igloo's door, he kicked a hole through the wall and peered anxiously within. "Uumayut!" he shouted exultantly. "They live"!

"As I looked into the gloomy chamber, I could make out four bodies, tucked in caribou skin blankets white with rime, curled up and huddled together with their heads turned toward the center of the igloo. The sole sign of life was their barely perceptible breathing.

"Weakened by near starvation, these people had eaten nothing but one fish in nine days. Toward the last they had devoured all but their most essential caribou skins. All the while the outside temperature had been 40° to 50°F below zero.

Marc Samgusak (Baker Lake, 1951)

"Later as our tea kettle warmed up on the Primus stove and one of them found speech, he first croak was not for food but a piteous cry of "Tipamik", tobacco!"

On March 21, 1951, the blowing snow was as violent as the day before, keeping the mission in complete isolation. What was there to do then, alone at home, beside reading, something Ataata Mary, always an avid reader, loved to do all day long, forgetting even at night to listen to the inter-missions broadcast. That very night, he did not forget and he received a message signed by Bishop Lacroix giving him a new obedience, this time for Repulse Bay.

At the end of March, Father Joseph Choque had returned from his holidays ready to hold again the reins of the mission. Bishop Lacroix himself had completed his official visit of Baker Lake and was anxious to proceed to Repulse Bay. There was no reason to postpone his departure except the fact that a few minutes before taking off, the pilot noticed that a support of the *Norseman* wing was broken and that the repair could not be done without first filling a pile of papers and waiting for a good mechanic to arrive from Churchill. The twin-engine airplane of the Arctic Wings Company arrived on April 7, bringing the repairman to Baker and left immediately, taking aboard Father Rousselière as far as Chesterfield and the Bishop to Churchill. Monseigneur Lacroix was really disappointed that he had been unable to reach Garry Lake. Father Buliard did not know what was delaying the Episcopal visit so long and he had to send back to their camps the Inuit who were impatiently expecting to be confirmed. At Chesterfield, Father Courtemanche and myself, Charles Choque, his assistant, were happy to welcome Father Mary-Rousselière. The next day, he presided at Sunday High Mass, a rare opportunity to see and hear such a congregation singing in unison Latin and Inuktitut hymns.

7

REPULSE BAY

After two weeks spent in Chesterfield, the very first mission of the Hudson Bay Vicariate, pleased to have seen the work accomplished by the Grey Nuns at the St.Thérèse Hospital, Father Rousselière left for Repulse Bay, April 21, 1951. Repulse Bay is called in Inuktitut, *Naujat*, with reference to the multitude of seagulls coming each summer from the south. There were only two passengers on the plane, Ataata Mary and the renowned photographer Richard Harrington. In search of unique Arctic scenes, he was en route to Pelly Bay planning to travel from Repulse to Pelly by dog team together with the Inuit who came to pick up the supplies destined for Father Vandevelde. Many of our missionaries owe to the ever observing camera of Richard Harrington their portraits in books and magazines.

The origin of the name *Repulse* is contested. Some say that it was given by an intrepid unknown captain of the early 18th century who, blocked by the ice, was obliged to turn back. So he called the Bay "*the one that repulses*". Others believe that the bay of Repulse was discovered in 1742 by Middleton patrolling the waters of the Hudson Bay aboard an English war vessel called the "*Repulse*". No matter what, the truth is that the ice in Repulse Bay is often the one element that commands the going and coming of boats.

Repulse Bay: Fathers Papion, Cochard, Guy Mary-Rousselière,
Didier and Paradis (in front)

Dr. John Rae became aware of this predicament when, in 1846, he sailed in the bay of Repulse on board his coaster. He settled at the mouth of the river that he baptized "*North Pole River*" and built himself a small house of stones joined together with clay and covered with walrus skin. Dr. Rae had at his service a crew of Montagnais. Being a volatile and stern man, he killed with one shot of his musket one of his Indian servants for stealing a goose from the pantry. Rae was also a great traveller and during the winter, he went around the country as far as Pelly Bay. The stories about Rae and the numerous whalers, who until the Great War sought fame and fortune in the Hudson Bay, were still vivid in the minds of the old Inuit when Father Emmanuel Duplain[1] visited them in 1925. He arrived by dog sled from Chesterfield with Henry Udjuk and Charles Innuksuk as his guides. Father Duplain stayed ten days at Repulse, as a guest of the Hudson Bay Company. He preached the gospel and took care of the sick, among them a small girl named Piuva whose belly and chest were frightfully burned.

In September 1931, Father Clabaut left the construction of the Chesterfield hospital and went to Repulse aboard the Company schooner, the *Fort Severn*. He was allowed to gather the Inuit in the store of the *Revillon Frères Company* where he conducted a service with sermon and hymns in Inuktitut. He also distributed holy pictures and miraculous medals. Everyone accepted them but some, as soon as they were outdoors, threw them to the wind!

In 1932, the same Father Clabaut, travelling this time by dog sled with Ayaruar and Kolit as his guides, made

---

[1] Emmanuel Duplain (1892-1972), French Canadian Oblate. He arrived in Chesterfield in 1921. A good seaman, he was on the *M.F. Therese* when the mission boat was shipwrecked at Cape Dorset in 1944. He died in the General Hospital in the city of Quebec where he had retired after ministering to the Manitoba Indians.

the trip together with the R.C.M.P. patrol. He arrived at Repulse on May 1 and put his Apostolate under the heavenly protection of the Virgin, *Our Lady of the Snows*. Back to Chesterfield by canoe on August 13, he learned that Bishop Turquetil had officially approved the foundation of a Catholic Mission at Repulse Bay, with himself in charge, starting in 1933.

When Father Mary-Rousselière arrived there on April 21, 1951, he found a very fervent Christian community almost equally divided between Anglicans and Catholics.

Father Theophile Didier[2] had been in charge of "*Our Lady of the Snows*" Mission since 1947. He spoke the Inuktitut language perfectly, he loved the people and was loved in return. Very level-headed, blessed with a sense of humour that helped him to accept without bitterness the craziest distractions, he will go down in history as one of the official translators of the Bible into Inuktitut.

On May 9, Father Rousselière stole a ride on Lionel Nutaradlaluk's sled and went to Lyons Inlet. There, he baptized the daughter of Hubert Amarualik who was a month old. Sometimes, on Sundays, he would walk from the post to visit the Inuit who were camped on the ice, hunting seal, and he would say mass for them. The ice was thick, solid, not like in November 1939 when his friend Father Buliard took an unwanted bath that almost cost him his life.

In September 1951, Father Rousselière took the opportunity to board the Igloolik Peterhead on its way to Chesterfield Inlet to pick up supplies for the mission.

---

[2] Theophile Didier (1910-1986), French Oblate, sent to the Arctic in 1935. He received in 1982, the "Commissioner's Award" for his contribution to the preservation of the Inuktitut language, his translations of the New Testament and his work among the Natives. In 1986, he was made "Doctor Honoris Causa" of the University of Toronto. The 12th of November 1986, he perished in a plane accident at Rankin Inlet.

He admitted that he was not as good a sailor as the Inuit but however that he did quite honourably!

On December 24, 1952, Richard Harrington had returned North to photograph the Native people. Father Rousselière saw him at work during the Christmas festivities. Too bad that he was not there a few days earlier to photograph, at *Naujadjuar*, the fire that destroyed in the morning old Pialak's house. It was made of canvas and moss and under the heavy weight of the snow, the roof had caved in, touching the flame of the seal-oil lamp. Inevitably the moss caught fire waking up Pialak and his wife who were still in bed. With no time to dress, they escaped covered only with a blanket and went to ask refuge at a neighbour's house.

The 5th of April 1953, Father Rogatien Papion[3] arrived from Pelly Bay by plane, on his way to civilization to consult an oculist. The reflection of the sun on the arctic snow is often very hard on the eyes. The Inuit themselves protected their eyes by wearing goggles or strips of wood, antler or bone which had a longitudinal slit in the center allowing them to see. Born a jack of all trades, Father Papion spent his time fixing things and visiting the camps before catching a plane for the continuation of his flight south.

Ataata Mary stayed at Repulse Bay until September 1953, together with Father Didier or alone during his superior's trip to Europe. He busied himself visiting the camps, hunting with the Inuit, fishing for arctic char, pulling out nets, following partridges, killing a bear which unfortunately fell in deep water, visiting the sick or

---

[3] Rogatien Papion, French Oblate, born in 1921, arrived North in 1947, lived in Thom Bay from 1949 to 1952, then went successively to Baker Lake, Arviat, Whale Cove, Rankin, Chesterfield, Repulse, etc. In 1996, he retired in Churchill, Manitoba, and later to the *Casa Bonita* in St. Boniface. Speaking Inuktitut fluently, he visits Inuit patients coming to Winnipeg for health care and makes periodic trips up North to assist in the missions.

Eskimo goggles

baptizing new born babies. At times, in summer, he simply sailed leisurely along the coast in a small sailboat searching for archaeological sites worthy of mention. The Assistant Director of the Museum of Man in Paris had advised him to write an article on the ancient sites that were discovered near Repulse Bay in order to make Ottawa more receptive to his request for an excavation permit.

Very early in the morning, on September 16, 1953, on the H.B.C. boat, the *Rupertsland,* Father Didier arrived back in Repulse coming from Rome where he had taken part in the General Chapter of the Oblates of Mary Immaculate.His return gave Father Mary-Rousselière liberty to leave. So in the evening, together with the medical team in charge of X-raying the Inuit, Ataata Mari took the *Rupertsland* on its way to Churchill where the Bishop was expecting him.

Churchill

Monseigneur Lacroix had given Father Rousselière an obedience for Churchill. This episcopal decision did not please him very much but being a good religious man, he accepted without making a fuss to be put in charge of the *Eskimo* magazine. He was certainly the most able candidate for the job. He brought down with him from the North much material concerning the country and its inhabitants. This included numerous photos and drawings of the Inuit that he had made himself. Such a source of documentation would facilitate his editorial work and allow him to offer the readers of the magazine well written and beautifully illustrated articles. However, he could not resist considering the fact that being so far away from the Inuit was a handicap, seriously limiting his knowledge of the life, culture and irreversible evolution of the nordic region.

He was to reside at Churchill from 1953 to 1958. But he was often seen in the North. On May 19, 1954, Father Jean-Marie Trébaol noted in the Igloolik journal the arrival of *Arctic Wings,* carrying on board Dr. Wood who had come to inoculate the Inuit against trichinosis as well as Father Rousselière and two geologists, Richard Emerik of New York and Jørgen Meldgaard, assistant curator of the Copenhagen National Museum.Together, with Pacôme Qulaut as guide, they visited old Eskimo houses and took photographs. They went to *Krikirtardjuk* where apparently, one could find traces of the Dorset culture. From June 20 to mid-August, they moved to *Alarniq* where they lived among the Inuit. Every morning, Ataata Mari celebrated Mass. In his report to Monseigneur Lacroix, Father Rousselière underlined the advantage of such expeditions: "Without mentioning some specific scientific results, I brought back with me abundant written and photographic documentation that has its usefulness for the editor of a magazine such as *Eskimo*. I have represented the Church in a field from where it is too often absent, especially in the North, that of ethnology. In acting this way, I did not believe that I was straying away from the directives of the Church. I was reading recently an account of a session on religious ethnology in which in a very special way, His Holiness insisted on the urgent necessity of studying closely certain aboriginal groups destined for extinction in the near future." The Inuit were certainly not destined for disappearance in the near future, but their ancestral way of life was threatened. On September 23, 1954, the three researchers left Igloolik on the Hudson Bay Company plane. At Repulse, Father Mary-Rousselière gave his seat on the plane to a sick Inuk and with Father Papion, continued to Chesterfield on Joseph Patterk's Peterhead. They arrived in time to celebrate the feast day of the Little Flower, the Patron Saint of the

Missions. From Chesterfield, Father Rousselière headed for Churchill on the first available plane.

On May 25, 1955, he landed at Baker Lake where I was posted and until the beginning of July kept me company. In June he pitched his tent with the Inuit camped at *Akkilasarjuk* for the spring fishing. Walking along the Prince River he discovered old campsites, traces of muskox and ancient traps made of stone. He crossed the lake on the ice to photograph the white geese at the mouth of the Kazan River. From July 9 to August 14, he was alone, until Father Rio came to join him as the new director of the Baker Lake mission. On the 16th, they sang together Requiem Mass for the repose of the soul of Bishop Turquetil. They had just learned of his death on June 14, 1955, in Washington. One day, walking along the Thelon River, Father Mary-Rousselière spent some time examining an old dwelling but without finding anything particularly interesting. "Our old Caribou Eskimos were nomads and did not leave behind many objects witnessing their passage", remarked Father Rio.

At the end of August, Father Mary-Rousselière went to Garry Lake aboard *Arctic Wings* and while the plane made several trips back and forth to bring supplies to the small mission, he chatted with Father Buliard, amazed at the exiguity and the poverty of the place. Together they went to see the nets and while Father Buliard was removing some white fish, Father Rousselière took photos of this daily, often hard and unpleasant chore.

On September 7, he definitively left Baker Lake with some American fishermen who were on their way to Chesterfield by plane. There he stayed and visited the sick at St. Therese's Hospital and with his Minifon recorder, saved from oblivion the stories of William Okkumaluk who had arrived from Igloolik with an injured foot.

Father Joseph Buliard in front of the Lady of the Rosary Mission in Garry Lake

Never did the Father waste his time, avid as he was to learn more and more of the Natives' past, their origins, their legends, and their customs. Very often he could be seen walking with his camera or his cine-camera in hand, trying to capture, on the spot, the activities of the school or the hospital.

On the 19th of September, he continued toward Churchill aboard the amphibious plane of the Foundation Company, the company who had the contract for building, at Chesterfield, a relay station linked with the Dew Line, a project that never materialized!

Conscious that photography is an art and that, in order to succeed, it is important to be well equipped, Father Mary-Rousselière went East to consult experts in the trade. Jean Roy, an employee of the National Film Board that he had known in the North, gave him important advice and some lighting material just as precious. He bought coloured film, a precision photometer and even a second hand Leica that was almost new. When in Ottawa, he consulted sound-specialists, wishing to transfer on regular records the Eskimo legends and songs that he had registered on his Minifon during the summer. He also brought to the National Museum of Man, the actual Museum of Civilization, an archaeological collection from Igloolik, and met many leading researchers and influential personalities. Thanks to Graham Rowley, he was able to obtain detailed maps of the North. At Montreal, he visited the Arctic Institute (which has since been transferred to Calgary), and met the linguist Gilles Lefebvre in charge of standardising the Inuktitut alphabet, and, besides all this, he found time to see his dentist.

On the way back by train to Churchill, he visited again the sanatoriums of Brandon and Clearwater Lake where many Inuit were treated for tuberculosis. Most of them were very lonely and all found the "white" food simply insipid.

8

PELLY BAY

The foundation of the "St. Pierre Mission" at Pelly Bay, *Arviliqjuar* in Inuktitut, goes back to Father Pierre Henry who on April 26, 1935, left Repulse Bay to settle among the *Netjilit*. The Breton missionary was heading for the unknown, but strong in his trust of the Lord, he resisted the temptation to turn back notwithstanding the great hardships suffered along the way.He was accompanying the Qasuvik family recently baptized at *Kursluk* by Father Clabaut. On May 31, from the top of the hills overlooking the *sapputit* or homemade stone weirs constructed to imprison the fish, he rejoiced to see on the horizon the islands of Pelly Bay, the very location of his forthcoming Apostolate. On June 10, living in a tent, he placed the cornerstone of his future chapel. During the winter however, he moved to an igloo heated with a primitive stone lamp burning seal or whale oil. Impressed by his reddish beard, the Inuit gave Father Henry the surname of *Kayualuk, the Red Bearded One.*

On April 23, 1938, Father Vandevelde, full of energy and missionary spirit, his face encircled by a beautiful black beard, came to put an end to Father Henry's solitary life.

On December 17, 1955, the temperature at Pelly Bay fell to 42° below zero Fahrenheit, the day Father Mary-Rousselière arrived there, loaded with the photographic equipment he hoped to use to film the life of

Guy Mary-Rousselière and the first Mission in Pelly Bay

the Inuit in winter. His confrère and friend Father Vandevelde was then alone in charge of the Mission dedicated to the Virgin of the Poor. Father Henry had decided to go further North. Ataata Vitipi or Vinivi as the Inuit called Father Vandevelde was managing, with an experienced hand, the destiny of the Pelly Bay people. He was also maintaining friendly relations with the people of the Dew Line, the nearest post being just a few kilometres from Pelly Bay, near *Tassiqjjuar*. He generously accommodated Father Rousselière, and did everything possible to facilitate his project. He supervised the construction of the *kaggik*, the big igloo which every year sheltered the Christmas festivities. The electric generator lent by the Dew Line and indispensable to the shooting of the film, refused, alas, to cooperate during the Holy Night! An emergency call was immediately made to Site 26 and on Christmas Day around noon there arrived at the Mission, Father Joseph Leverge[1] accompanied by several men of the Dew Line. Among the visitors were two mechanics who quickly checked the wiring, verified the contacts, cleansed the gas line and restored life to the stubborn generator. Young dogs were sitting by, watching the rescue operation with a mischievous look and as soon as the motor turned and was left without supervision, they came running and played with the wires, causing a short-circuit plunging the assembly in darkness and putting to the test the patience of the film producer! The midnight Mass in the igloo cathedral, the banquet, the games, the sled races, nothing escaped the ever-vigilant eye of the camera. Father Rousselière even attempted, from a large heated box,

---

[1] Joseph Leverge, Oblate missionary, born in France in 1924, arrived in the North in 1949, spent many years in *Talujjar* (Spence Bay), then Rankin Inlet. He left the Inuit missions in 1978 to join the western Oblates of St. Paul Province.

to capture the magnificence of the polar night and the ever-changing arabesques of the blowing snow.

On January 12, 1956, he photographed the baptism of Fabien Oogak's child born the night before, to whom, in sign of his friendship for Ataata Mari, Father Vandevelde gave the name of Guy-Marie. On the 25th, Father Rousselière left Pelly Bay for Site 26. After many days of waiting at the Dew Line, he reached Churchill on February 10. Father Vandevelde wrote in the Pelly Bay Codex that, in spite of the absent-mindedness of his visitor, he really missed his congenial company.

He will not miss it very long because on March 3, 1956, after collecting articles for the next two issues of the *Eskimo* and having had his photographic equipment treated to resist low temperatures, he flew back to Site 26 and from there proceeded to Pelly Bay by dog sled. The well marked path leading from the Site to the settlement was sometimes scary, going down abrupt slopes or zigzagging between rocks. At strategic points on the trail, statues of the Virgin Mary, planted solidly on empty oil barrels, were inviting the travellers to stop and to pray an Ave Maria. The *kaggik*, built for Christmas, was still standing. The following day the Inuit assembled there for the Easter banquet and were offered all the specialties of the country: Arctic char —the best of its kind—caribou—half frozen or boiled— served with hard biscuits and black tea. Father Rousselière completed the film *The Life of a Small Eskimo Girl* with Sarakuluk as the star. He filmed the seal hunt *"aux aglus"*, the holes in the ice where the seals come to breathe, with Bernard Iqugaqtuq as the hunter; the native dance with Niptayok as the drummer and other scenes that will make up the missionary film of which he dreamed. He regretted not having been able to film *The Day of an Eskimo Boy* because his camera had caused him trouble. On May 20,

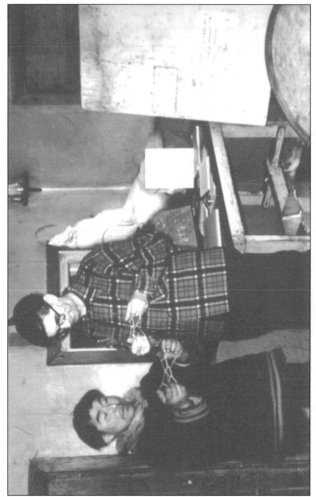

String games with Guy Mary-Rousselière and Bernard Iqugaqtuq (Pelly Bay)

via the Dew Line, he visited Cambridge Bay, then King William but he missed Father Henry. "It is unimaginable to put out a film on Pelly Bay without at least showing the face of Father Henry", he wrote to Bishop Lacroix. From Gjoa Haven to Spence and from Spence to Pelly, he travelled with some Inuit. The weather was so beautiful that somewhere on the road he removed his *kolliktar* and his outer caribou pants and lost them. He arrived at Father Vandevelde's on June 18. The hard frozen ground was starting to thaw allowing him to start without delay his archaeological excavations accompanied by the irritating buzzing of hungry mosquitoes. On July 31, about an hour's ride from the mission, beyond *Irkalulik* Lake, he discovered a four thousand year old pre-Dorset camp! On August 13, at *Isurtuk,* he made discoveries dating back to the Tunit period. Between his excavating sessions, taking advantage of the open water, he filmed the Inuit in their kayaks. Everywhere and for everything, he could count on the generous and expert help of Bernard Iqugaqtuq, a living example of the resourcefulness of the Eskimos which Ataata Mari admired without reservation.

The violent snowstorm of August 31, was unable to spoil his happiness when he returned to the mission having discovered a beautiful small stone mask on the hill of *Kugarjuk*. That turned out to be his last exploration of the season.

On September 15, with winter around the corner, he left Pelly Bay and on the 19th arrived at Churchill, where a huge pile of mail was waiting for him. He learned the sad news that his mother was to undergo a kidney removal and he greatly worried until the day he knew that the operation had been a success.

Back at Pelly Bay in December 1956, after a few recordings and the filming of an unsuccessful and cold polar bear hunt, he went to Hall Beach via the Dew Line, and from there, with the wind in his face and a 40° below zero weather, he left by dog sled for Igloolik. On the eve of Christmas, he entertained the Inuit, showing them slides from his enormous collection. During the Midnight Service, that he partly filmed and recorded, he found that Father Fournier's choir was excellent, singing *con brio* Inuktitut hymns as well as the Latin ordinary of the Mass. Putting his camera aside, Father Mary played the harmonium during the Solemn Mass of Christmas day, revealing his talent as a musician. Then followed the dried beans banquet cooked in a huge pot and enjoyed thoroughly by the 130 Inuit present. In the afternoon, the Benediction of the Blessed Sacrament, enhanced by a solemn *Tantum Ergo* in two parts, was followed by traditional games and the distribution of gifts. On the 27th, Father Rousselière recorded on the Minifon some *A-ya-ya* from Ludger Otak, Jean-Marie Anangoar and Kulliktalik. The following day, he left Igloolik for Site 30, hoping to reach Churchill in time to celebrate New Year.

He did not make it and his landing at the Gate of the North on January 3, 1957, coincided with the news concerning Father Buliard's tragic disappearance in Garry Lake. Being rather an introvert, Guy kept within himself the deep sorrow caused by his friend's untimely death. He had the painful duty to pass along the sad news to all the Fathers of the Vicariate through the *Northern Messenger* weekly broadcasting. For the readers of *Eskimo,* after having announced briefly the tragic event in the March issue, in the following issue he traced a moving portrait of Joseph Buliard, great missionary among the *Sanningayuligmiut* of the Back River, a true missionary "who took very seriously his own life, his calling to the priesthood, the Gospel, but without ever taking himself too seriously". Brought up in the Franche-Comté region, close to the beautiful valley of the Doubs, not far from Switzerland, he came from a family "where Christian virtues were far from morose and where joy was always ready to explode". He had eleven brothers and sisters, all trained to work, to love their work and to do it well. Joseph was an average student, very strict with himself, fond of silence. His missionary vocation surprised no one, and in June 1939, he received his obedience for the Hudson Bay Vicariate. It is easy to follow year after year Father Buliard's life in the Great North through the *Eskimo* magazine. Just the titles of the articles speak loudly. For instance: *Journeying with Christ in the Arctic,* where we read about Father Buliard's stay in Wager and his first visit to the Back River. *Paradise without Lice or Darkness* which narrates, in the region of Aberdeen Lake, the baptism of Kublu, an old tattooed and decrepit lady whose soul became purified and embellished by the grace of the sacrament. Both accounts, *Christ at Garry Lake* and *Traveller for Christ in the Barrenlands,* contain long and pertinent extracts of the Garry Lake Mission diary, a friendly homage from Father Mary-Rousselière to Father Joseph Buliard.

The Film Maker

The year 1957 saw the production of the film *Lux in Tenebris (Light in the darkness)*. It was realized and edited in Hollywood. To be near the studio, Father Rousselière boarded with the Oblates of San Fernando or at Saint Peter's rectory, on the outskirts of Beverley Hills. He rubbed shoulders with the famous names of show business such as Thom Fox, Larry Crosby, Jack Douglas and many others, trying to keep pace with them. "I have come to the conclusion", he wrote to Bishop Lacroix on July 15, 1957, "that in Hollywood, the virtue of patience is as important as it is in Eskimo country". To pay off in part the expenses of the film production and, by the same token, acquaint people with the Northern Missions, he arranged short showings for television entitled: *The Priest of Pelly Bay*. The text was in English, although his intention was also to have the French version of the film made in Hollywood, for reasons of economy. Luckily, moneywise, Bishop Lacroix was behind him. In September, the script having been recorded and the work being well advanced, Father Rousselière went to France. After a long wait, and a resulting severe insomnia, a copy of the film *Lux in Tenebris* finally reached him, the definitive version and commentaries but still without any musical background. He made up for it by using a record player to diffuse an appropriate music when showing the film to the public.

Father Rousselière rejoiced to be with his family, especially to find his mother in good health. In order to visit, in her company, the relatives living at the four corners of the country, he learned how to drive a car and rented a small automobile from the Oblates in Paris. The 2 CV was also very convenient to transport all the necessary equipment that he had bought for the projection of his film. He had posters printed in three colours to announce the place and the time of the show. He went to many Oblate communities, various parochial halls and even to the Museum of Man in Paris. Responding to Father General's personal invitation, in January 1958, he travelled to Rome and presented his film to the members of the Oblate General Administration. In the Vatican, he showed it at the Propaganda Palace before Monsignor Sigismondi and his collaborators. He wrote Bishop Lacroix in whom he always found an understanding Superior, that "One of the most sympathetic audiences was the one at the Arctic Institute of Copenhagen". Among the viewers were members of the

Greenlandic Administration with their Chief; the Admiral of the Danish Fleet and famous ethnologists. Everyone agreed that the film was the best they had seeen on the Arctic. At the end of the performance, Captain Ejnar Mikkelsen, the Greenland Inspector, came to congratulate him and, shaking his hand, he said that he would like to show the film to all the Pastors in Greenland and let them see the admirable work of the Catholic Missionaries among the Canadian Inuit. Helge Larsen, president of the Arctic Institute, ordered a copy of the English version of the film, hoping Father Mary would come in person to present it to a much larger audience.

Back in Hollywood about mid-April, he discussed a few small changes in the film and paid the overdue bills. All in all, he was satisfied with his visit in the illustrious city of show business, in spite of a few little things in need of more attention, for example, the title and the credits to be mentioned at the beginning of the film.

9

BEYOND THE HIGH HILLS

On July 27, 1958, in Churchill, he boarded the
C. D. Howe heading for Pond Inlet. On board, a representative of Northern Affairs confided to him that soon
the Government would bring Inuit from diverse northern
localities to Grise Fiord. Father Rousselière did not suspect
that about thirty-five years later this policy although drawn
primarily for the welfare of the indigenous people, would
bring on the Canadian Government an accusation of
genocide and cost the Canadian taxpayers millions of
dollars in compensation. On August 7, he arrived
at Resolute Bay and from there, on August 18, aboard the
ice-breaker *Labrador,* he reached Pond Inlet, his final
destination, where he intended to stay for an indefinite time.
Father Jean Dufour[1], the residing priest since May 1956
welcomed him. The mission building was old and cold,
especially Father Rousselière's quarters upstairs. He
somewhat raised the temperature of his room by
lengthening the stove pipe coming from downstairs.

---

[1] Jean Dufour, born in 1928, French Oblate from the Diocese of Annecy.
He was ordained a priest by Bishop Clabaut and sent to the Northern
mission of Canada, Pond Inlet, Igloolik, Churchill and Iqaluit. Very
competent in audio-visual techniques, he produced some videos on the
Northern Missions. Because of illness, he left Iqaluit in 1995 and died at
Quebec on March 13, 1996.

In November, when the sun disappeared totally from the horizon, Father Mary-Rousselière, in agreement with Constable Dale Nelson, filmed the shark fishing. He took very beautiful photographs with, as background, the three icebergs immobilized in front of the settlement. Later he wrote an interesting article in *Eskimo*, September 1959, on shark fishing in Pond Inlet, illustrated with a picture of Constable Nelson looking at a frozen shark much taller than himself. He reminded the readers that there are many species of sharks and that the voracity of these sea-rovers is well known by the Inuit of the north-eastern coast of Baffin Land. It is even said that a human leg, together with its seal skin boot, was found in the stomach of a captured shark. Whether true or legendary, this macabre discovery, more than a hundred years old, does not fit the habit of the blue shark, the one who loves the very cold waters of the Arctic and furnishes two products whose commercial value is recognized. From its enormous liver, oil rich in vitamin A is extracted and its skin makes high quality shagreen. The Canadian Eskimos did not consider the shark as a game worthy of being hunted, even though they sometimes used its dried skin as a wood scraper or a scratcher to soften the caribou skins. Attempts at shark fishing conducted in the winter of 1957 at the Government's request by the Mounted Police of Pond Inlet were conclusive. Many were captured in a few days with a fish hook about 10 cm. long, baited with a piece of seal and lowered almost to the floor of the sea. The shark taken by Constable Nelson and Father Mary measured over two metres and when hooked, did not offer much resistance. The shark has no bones, but only cartilage. The extreme ruggedness of its skin did not stop the young dogs who followed the fishermen to devour some of the meat without any ill effects, even though it is said that the flesh of the shark is very toxic. The results of this experience were rather positive but will the Government facilitate shark fishing and thus encourage the exploitation of an abundant natural resource, the future will tell.

In March 1959, the Pond Inlet Mission, where the ministerial work, according to Father Rousselière's expression, did not overwork the missionaries, was temporarily closed. Father Dufour left on the R.C.M.P. plane for Igloolik via Frobisher Bay, the pilot having kindly given him a seat. As for Father Rousselière, he left by dog sled for *Nunasiar* where he celebrated Easter with the Inuit before continuing on to Igloolik on April 1st with Maktar, Thomasi and Utuwak. This was an 18 day trip done in many stages and made pleasant by a successful caribou hunt. At *Ikirtak* Lake, Alain built an *inuksuk* to serve as a beacon for dog teams coming from Igloolik to meet them.

At *Ikpiardjuk*, Father Rousselière discovered a whole Oblate community made of Danielo, Fournier and Dufour. The first had a bad cough and experienced many sleepless nights; in fact he was sick enough to be soon evacuated to the south. The other two priests, remote successors of the monks of the Middle Ages, builders of beautiful cathedrals, were constructing a low-rise stone church familiarly referred to as the *Ikpiardjuk Basilica*.

Chesterfield—Churchill

On May 28, 1959, *Arctic Wings* flew the children of Turquetil Hall to Igloolik for their holidays. Father Mary-Rousselière took advantage of the return trip to reach Chesterfield. He found the Sisters in jubilation, proud of their foundress, Marguerite d'Youville, who had been beatified on May 3rd. He entrusted the nurses of Saint Therese Hospital with a handicapped child named Ténénan that accompanied him from Igloolik. He no doubt was full

145

The Igloolik "Basilica"

of admiration for the devotedness of these "Heroic Women". However, deep down inside his heart, he was dreaming of a native community of sisters somewhat similar to the *Sisters of Our Lady of the Snows* founded by the Ursulines in Alaska.

On June 2, he reached Churchill and aware of his responsibility as editor of *Eskimo*, he started writing some thought-provoking articles on contemporary subjects such as medical care given to the Eskimos or the complex question of their education.

According to his research, medical care received by the Inuit left much to be desired. He wondered why the doctor in charge of the Catholic Hospital at Chesterfield had not been replaced. This well equipped institution was capable of taking adequate care of the sick instead of sending them south, far away from their home country. To justify this regretful decision to leave Chesterfield without a doctor, the government pointed out the presence of medical facilities in Churchill or the annual visit of the *Eastern Arctic Patrol* in most of the arctic settlements. The relative proximity of Churchill and the few hours of attention accorded each year to the Inuit by a group of doctors travelling by boat or plane was pitifully insufficient, especially during winter, the time of the most severe epidemics. Concerning nurses, male or female, in charge of the new nursing stations built by the government, he reproached them for not making home visits to the sick as the policemen and missionaries used to do. The patients had to go to the nursing station often under unacceptable travelling conditions. He insisted that, in fact, the Eskimo had the right to receive medical care in his own country, in a familiar environment and by a personnel that understood him. He also insisted that the local doctor, and not Ottawa bureaucrats, should have the authority to solve medical problems. The local doctor should be allowed to communicate by radio to the settlements under his jurisdiction and to give Eskimos living in faraway camps, elementary notions of hygiene and first aid. As to the young students, boys or girls, interested in pursuing a health related career, they should be allowed to become auxiliary nurses or even graduate nurses. Concerning Chesterfield Hospital, he denied strongly any Catholic "brain washing" on patients of a different denomination. Anglicans and all unbaptized Inuit were all cared for as well as any other sick person and once healed, were often full of admiration for the dedication of the Sisters. While acknowledging the fact that the government did pay a daily pension for an hospitalized Eskimo, he did not accept, figures in hand, the rumour saying that the mission was taking advantage of this policy to enrich itself at the expense of the taxpayers. While the hospital in Chesterfield was only receiving $7.00 a day per person, the fee was $21.00 per day at the hospital in Frobisher Bay, even for a new born baby. In concluding the preceding comments, he highlighted the generosity of the missionaries who took care of their flock without pay and did not hesitate to visit the sick in the most remote Inuit camps.

Concerning educational issues relating to the Inuit, Father Rousselière refuted a biased article written by Farley Mowat, the well known author and supposed expert on Eskimo matters. Mr. Mowat had accused the Catholic missionaries of having kept in isolation the population of the North for more than a hundred years when the truth was that the first mission in the Central Arctic located at Chesterfield Inlet was only founded in 1912. He also stated that these same missionaries had prevented the Inuit from learning one of the two national languages. To this accusation, Father Rousselière shrewdly remarked that if the Inuit had learned French, a cry of Nationalism would have been heard across the nation! Was it not to the credit of the Oblates to have taught in Inuktitut, thereby contributing to the survival of the native tongue as well as to the preservation of the Eskimo culture with its three main components, hunting, fishing and trapping? The Inuktitut language was not to be compared to an old garment that should be thrown out but it was so much more; it had a role to play in the intellectual evolution of the North. All were invited to keep a legitimate pride of their heritage and to keep alive their own language; the children were also given the possibility of learning English, and later the opportunity to further their education.

Father Rousselière's editorials created more and more sensation among the people who were interested in the Inuit. His articles were based on solidly supported affirmations and they were written in a flexible and vivid style. They expressed a genuine interest towards the Native people and fearlessly criticized, directly but politely, certain authors who attacked the missions. He usually kept the last pages of the magazine for general news on the Arctic missions. As editor, his only criticism was that the English translation did not always completely express the original ideas of the French text. Time and time again, he insisted on the cooperation he was hoping to receive from his confrères, articles or photographs, but, alas, too often he knocked at a closed door!

Pond Inlet

On September 1, 1959, Father Mary-Rousselière arrived at Pond Inlet aboard the *C. D. Howe* coming from Churchill. During the trip, Dr. Lawrence Oschinsky from the National Museum in Ottawa had offered trips aboard the ship's helicopter to fly over the settlements the boat had to visit, Coral Harbour, Cape Dorset, Lake Harbour, Resolute, Arctic Bay and Grise Fjord. Once back at Mittimatalik, Ataata Mari had to store away the material unloaded from the boat. The season was late. He lost no time installing a new chimney on the mission and at the same time he repaired the roof, quite a risky task because of the freezing weather. On the 14th, in spite of the wind and moving ice, he went by canoe to *Nunasiar* where Alain Maktar and in fact the near totality of Catholic Inuit had their camp. Regardless of the bad weather and the snow starting to fall, the priest built a small shelter that he pompously named *Saint-Francis-of-Assisi Mission.* Measuring three metres by four, it was made of plywood and the interior walls were insulated with old newspapers or empty coal bags covered with white canvas bought from the Bay store. A small corner of the building served as chapel, just large enough for the Father to kneel in front of the Blessed Sacrament. A generator provided light for him and the two small Eskimo shacks near by. All around the building, in order to provide better protection from the wind, he had added blocks of peat moss. Alain proved to be a very good helper and he was also an excellent hunter. On the 19th of September, he killed five narwhals, one with a set of double tusks which would be sent to museum in Churchill. On November 30, Alain accompanied Father Rousselière to Pond Inlet where on December 15, by moonlight, the mail was parachuted. On the 21st, in spite of a violent storm, Father and Alain returned to *Nunasiar.* The route was so bad that the sled toppled over and Father lost his glasses. At *Nunasiar,* he celebrated Christmas in the intimacy of his small Catholic community. During the week, he gathered the children to teach them catechism while the men went visiting their seal nets. For some reason, and to his great disappointment, he was unable to receive any radio

Alain Maktar, an excellent hunter

message from Igloolik or from Churchill, although he succeeded to stay in daily contact with the R.C.M.P., at Pond Inlet. The year ended with a strong blizzard and a temperature so low that the mass wine froze in the bottles. Comfortably warm in their thick fur, the Arctic hares did not mind either snow or cold and, at the risk of their lives, were leaving their tracks all around the settlement. On February 6, on Bylot Island, one could observe the pale reflection of the sun and rejoice at the first sign of the polar night coming gradually to an end.

On March 18, at 40° below zero weather, Father Rousselière returned to Mittimatalik. There, on April 7, he received his mail by a Nordair plane bringing supplies for a team of surveyors soon to come in the area. On April 12, he left Pond Inlet for Arctic Bay and Igloolik by dog sled together with Alain and his children, except for the youngest one who was entrusted to the grandmother. They arrived at their destination on May 16.

At the beginning of June 1960, Father Mary-Rousselière went from Igloolik to Foxe Main, on the Dew Line, and there he lived under a tent. The dentist at the base agreed to treat some of his teeth that had been damaged, eating frozen meat. He later went to Pelly Bay where he met Doug Wilkinson, former government official, film producer and pilot of his own Piper Cub. Having difficulties with his Minifon recorder, Father borrowed from Doug a portable tape recorder that Asen Balikci had left him and was thus able to continue his recordings. On September 19, from the Dew Line, he wrote to the Bishop in Churchill asking permission to go to Montreal to buy new eye glasses having lost not only one but the two extra pairs he kept carefully in case of bad luck!

Passing through Frobisher, he learned—news confirmed later by a Police report—that the carpenters hired by the

Department of Northern Affairs to build a new school at Pond Inlet, had broken into the mission and had drunk the four or five gallons of sacramental wine. It was also reported to him that these undesirables had made some homemade booze and as a predictable consequence of drunkenness had invited the Inuit to drink, in the meantime raping two young girls of 15 or 16 years of age. It was also said that they were bargaining with the Eskimos, exchanging government property for bear skins or fox pelts which were easily hidden in the midst of their luggage. Finally, the plane came after much delay to evacuate them back to the South.

After staying awhile in Ottawa to add a few artifacts to the Museum Collection and to consult archaeological books, Ataata Mary returned to the North and spent Christmas at Pelly Bay. In April 1961, he returned to Igloolik where he attempted to bring a happy conclusion to a complicated marriage between a young girl of the area and an Inuk resident of Pond Inlet. The girl's parents were not pleased to see their daughter depart for Pond Inlet. With perfect diplomacy, Ataata Mari promised them that the following spring she would come to visit them and their decision to keep their daughter wavered, at least momentarily. The coming of this young couple was a welcome addition to the small catholic community of Pond. However, according to Father, the small number, or even the complete absence of faithful, should never be a reason to close a mission. "At the scholasticate, they would tell us that we were not only going to the far away missions to convert souls but to 'implant' the Church. The Church has indeed taken roots in Pond Inlet even if it still has the dimensions of a small shoot. I am not one of those who advise to uproot it." This he wrote June 14, 1961, from Churchill where he had arrived at the beginning of the month.

Father Mary-Rousselière was too much attracted to Pond Inlet not to go back. Aboard the *C. D. Howe,* under the direction of Captain Ouellette, he left Churchill July 30. The ship stopped at the settlements along the coast. The Medical Patrol headed by Dr. Herman went ashore aboard the ship's helicopter repatriating the Inuit back from the sanatoriums, examining the local people and evacuating new cases of tuberculosis. Between Resolute Bay and Pond Inlet, the helicopter tried to reach a few Inuit camps but to no avail, the wind made it turn back, a wind so strong that the waves even destroyed three canoes on the boat's bridge.

The *C. D. Howe* stopped at *Nunasiar* on August 19 and unloaded the supplies for the Saint Francis Mission before continuing to Pond Inlet. Major d'Artois, Chief of the "Rangers" was also on board. He was the one who parachuted at Moffet in 1947 to rescue Canon Turner after his fatal accident. There was also on board a team from Radio Canada who had filmed a walrus hunt at Grise Fjord, and three carpenters, a Canadian, a Scot and a Bavarian who would build the administrator's house in Pond.

Father's return had been approved by his superiors and he was happy to be back looking after his small Catholic congregation. His mind was preoccupied with his scientific projects that were partially subsidized by government organizations. In order to facilitate management of his finances, he asked the bursar of the Vicariate to open a bank account in his name, something so far unheard of for a member of a religious community with vow of poverty.

Southern civilization was introducing itself rapidly at Mittimatalik. A school had been officially opened in March 1961 and coming from distant camps, many children boarded in the village in order to attend the new school, a solution that did not please all the parents, because of the lack of supervision. A mining company settled at Strathcona Sound

Inuit transported to the boat for medical checkup

and intensifying the drilling, had plans to go as deep as 2,000 feet. The majority of the personnel were white but many Inuit would soon find work there and, hopefully, in a less negatively influenced atmosphere than the one at Frobisher Bay. According to rumours, alcohol flowed a bit too liberally in Frobisher Bay causing hardship and filling up the prison. Father Rousselière was horrified by alcoholism. He even refused to make sacramental wine with dried raisins as some of his confrères did, afraid to induce the Inuit to do the same for their own consumption.

Father Mary would rather work at some intellectual task. In 1961, a book of poems by Knud Rasmussen that was illustrated with photographs by Father Rousselière was published in the United States. This title *Beyond the High Hills* was reviewed in the St. Petersburg Times, October 22 with the following note: "Perhaps best suited for ages six to ten, *Beyond the High Hills* can be for any age. It will be unfortunate if Eskimo poetry has limited appeal, for this is one of the best and most unusual books of the year, with strikingly beautiful color photos by Guy Mary-Rousselière. School and town libraries should have it, as should homes in which there is a desire for beautiful books." The following year Father Mary received a note from the Editor of Children's Books: "Just a note to let you know that *Beyond the High Hills* has just been chosen by the American Library Association here as one of their list of forty-six Notable Children's Books published during 1961. This list is a very important one and highly selective."

In September, at *Nunasiar*, he enlarged the mission, installed the transmitter Marconi CN 26 that Captain Dufour of the icebreaker *Iberville* had delivered by helicopter. To his great delight, he contacted first Gjoa Haven and Repulse Bay, then Chesterfield and Churchill where Father Danielo answered him in Inuktitut. He told them of the narwhals and seals that were abundant in the sea, frolicking around a huge iceberg immobilized in front of the camp. At the end of October, everything was frozen and the sun disappeared for good. The trapping season was about to begin and woe to the foxes reckless enough to approach the caches where walrus meat, seal blubber or fish had been stored; they were all encircled by traps whose deadly teeth were ready to close in, irremediably, on the paw that will touch the trigger.

On December 8, a solemn day for the Oblates, a day dedicated to Mary Immaculate, their patroness, Father Rousselière arrived at Pond Inlet by dog team. He found the mission to be a real icebox. A stove and two Primus lamps were barely able to heat properly the kitchen before he decided to return to *Nunasiar* for the Christmas celebrations. A stomach ache, luckily not too serious, forced him to begin the year 1962 in bed.

On February 10, at -40° C, the sun appeared for five minutes at noon, between two mountains. On February 20, John Glenn was orbitting the earth in a space capsule and what pleased Father Rousselère just as much, Alain came back from Pond Inlet with mail delivered earlier by the R.C.M.P. plane. On the 26th, Bob Pilot in charge of the Pond Inlet detachment, visited him and gave him all the local news. Bob was on his way to Arctic Bay, travelling by dog team, sleeping in igloos. At the end of March, one of these travelling igloos would offer a shelter to Father Rousselière on his way back to Pond Inlet where he waited for coming of spring and arrival of the aeroplane.

On April 29, he was finally able to reach Sannerajak (Hall Beach), and on May 4, left for Pelly Bay, Spence Bay, Gjoa Haven, Baker Lake and finally the next morning, to Chesterfield where the annual Oblate retreat had already started, preached by Father Jean Larvor, a French Oblate from the diocese of Quimper. On May 7, another Frenchman, Father Robert Haramburu, missionary in the Mackenzie, was transferred to the Hudson Bay Vicariate and was named Provincial Vicar. During the study sessions that followed the retreat, Father Rousselière and myself were designated as special reporters. At the conclusion of all these days of prayer and exchange, the golden jubilee of *Our Lady of La Delivrande Mission (1912-1962)* was celebrated with solemnity, heightened by the presence of many bishops and dignitaries. Nevertheless, what was most pleasant for the missionaries arriving from isolated posts was to be among their confrères and to share with them their northern adventures, their apostolic joys, and sometimes their defeats. Two of the first Inuit baptized in Chesterfield in 1917 were present, Marguerite Kralalak and John Ayaruar.

On May 18, Father Mary-Rousselière went to Igloolik. He boarded the *DC3* that was bringing home for their holidays, 25 children from the Chesterfield boarding school. He spent about ten days in the company of Fathers Haramburu and Fournier. He did not refuse to lend a helping hand to them and even made a successful batch of bread. From there, he went to Frobisher Bay, wanting to see for himself this community whose reputation was not always without blemish. He then returned to Sannerajak where an epidemic of trichinosis, immediately followed by the measles, had caused several deaths. It was not by any means the best time to visit the people. Grabbing the opportunity of a free ride to Pelly Bay, he flew there unannounced and remained with Father Vandevelde from June 30 to July 19, before finally returning to Pond Inlet, passenger on a plane of Lamb Airways chartered by the Geodesic Service. He was eager to resume his archaeological research.

Guy Mary-Rousselière making bread
(Photo Richard Harrington—Repulse Bay)

In August, with Alain Maktar, he continued the excavations at Button Point. This area was traditionally the most important winter and spring campsite for the Tununirmiut[2]. The weather being unfavourable, they moved to *Niaqongut* where they discovered vestiges of Dorset and Thule cultures.

University of Montreal

On September 2, 1962, Father Mary acquired accommodation on the *C. D. Howe* and went south to attend courses at the University of Montreal. He felt that he was somewhat old to go back to school and was afraid that, by being away too long, he would lose contact with the North. But encouraged by the Superior General, and egged on by researchers such as Asen Balikci and other museums specialists, he registered himself for a course in Anthropology leading to a Master's degree. According to the list he received, he would have to read 106 books in preparation for the final exams. There was really very little time left for him to do anything else although he insisted on visiting the Inuit hospitalized in the city, not wanting his studies to draw him away from his missionary ideal. Attending university had for him no other purpose than to serve the Inuit better. He worked hard and he succeeded fully. He obtained an average of 83.2%, 30 credits and the congratulations of his professor for having the highest marks in his class.

The university year being very short, on June 8, 1963, he had already returned to Pond Inlet in the plane of

---

[2] According to Father Mary-Rousselière, the Tununirmiut, when they arrived at Button Point sometime in June, hunted seals at breathing holes and along the floe edge where they also exploited narwhal and Greenland whale. As the ice receded into Eclipse Sound this group moved westward hunting *ujjuk* (the bearded seal) while in the spring some elements would cross Lancaster Sound for polar bear or muskoxen on north Devon Island.

Guy Mary-Rousselière receiving his Canadian Citizenship
from Bob Pilot, R.C.M.P., at Pond Inlet

Murray Watts, a very successful and generous prospector, with Ron Sheardon as pilot. He discovered that a new Catholic family had increased the number of his followers. In all aspects, Pond Inlet was becoming every day more important. Arts and crafts were developing. A considerable bed of iron had been discovered about a hundred miles to the southwest, near Lake *Inuktorvik,* that could provide a job to all the Inuit ready to work.

Due to a grant of $420.00 dollars from the National Museum in Ottawa, he hired Alain Maktar and Juupi Inurak to take him to Button Point. On the way, Juupi's sled fell in a crack on the sea. They had to camp in order to dry the skins and the supplies. The next day, Juupi returned to Pond Inlet with all the dogs. Ataata Mari, Alain and his family kept on going by canoe. They saw two huge whales, many white whales, walruses and some seals sleeping on the sea ice. The weather was cold with fog and snow. In mid-July, the geese flew over the camp. Alain Maktar shot four. As for the excavation, it progressed at the same rhythm as the thawing of the ground. Except for a pipe stem with the inscription *"S. Mc Lean, Dundee",* they made no sensational discovery.

On July the 31st, they all returned to Pond, stopping at Beloeil Island and at *Nutarasunniq,* reaching the mission on August 1st. The *Mischief,* a small boat coming from England, had already dropped anchor in the bay. The owner, Major Tillman, at his own request, had been put ashore with one other man north of Bylot, planning to cross Bylot Island on foot via the glaciers.

Back home, Father Rousselière acknowledged once again the lamentable state of his living quarters. They were in such a miserable condition that he thought it would be preferable to build anew. If only his Bishop would come to be aware of the situation!

Alain Maktar showing results of the excavation

10

A SKIDOO ACCIDENT

Pelly Bay

On August 22, Father Mary had an opportunity to go to Hall Beach; then he hopped aboard the plane transporting the children of Turquetil Hall to Chesterfield and went to Pelly Bay. Father Henry, founder of the Pelly Bay mission was also on the plane. Now old and grey-haired, but still with his piercing clear eyes, he was very happy to greet his former parishioners the short time the plane remained on ground.

Father Rousselière was to team up with Asen Balikci and Doug Wilkinson who had arrived there at the end of July. The latter had landed his small plane on a temporary runway, hand-shovelled by Father Vandevelde and a few Inuit and located at *Awatarpivik,* an island situated opposite the mission. This island was formerly an ideal camp ground whose name probably came from *awatarpait,* the seal skins containers in which seal oil was preserved. Father Rousselière, excavating on this island, found many interesting artifacts. Wilkinson and Balikci had as their main objective to film the real Eskimo life before it was forgotten even by the Natives. Zacharie Ittimangnerk and his family would play the main role in the film with

Fabien Oogak—Pelly Bay

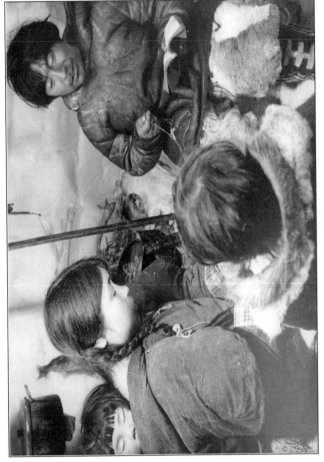

Bernard Iqugaqtuq—Pelly Bay

Fabien Oogak and Bernard Iqugaqtuq as assistants. With their wives and children, all will be excellent actors for depicting current activities of a family, camps, travel, bear hunt or fishing at the *sapputit,* particularly good during this season. Father Vandevelde's presence was invaluable to the producers and greatly facilitated their dealings with the autochtons. Father Mary-Rousselière himself served as an interpreter as he spoke the indigenous language perfectly. Also, more importantly, he had a deep knowledge of the Inuit, their culture, their history, their habits, their legends, their migrations as well as the ancestral tools for hunting and fishing. Therefore, he could give pertinent advice regarding the sequences of the filming.

Doug Wilkinson's plane damaged when he made a landing on rough terrain and had to remain grounded until repairs could be made. Not feeling too well, Doug decided to go South on the same plane that brought in Ataata Mari. His absence lasted until September 14. On August 25, it was Balikci's turn to leave Pelly Bay but not without having discussed at length his cinematographic work with Father Rousselière. The latter being alone went to the *sapputit* to complete filming fishing with the *"kakiwak",* a fish spear made of a long handle terminated by a metal spike between two barbed prongs which prevent harpooned fish from escaping. He was also very much interested in the string games of the *Arviligjuarmiut* in preparation for a book that eventually would be published in 1969 by the National Museum of Canada.

To facilitate his travelling, Father Rousselière had ordered a *skidoo* through the Dew Line. Skidoo or ski-doo is the popular name for a kind of snowmobile built by the famous Bombardier Company of Quebec and moving on a central track with two skis in front to ensure the proper direction. On October 21, proudly mounting his machine, he went to *Kungaardjuk* about fifty kilometres from the mission, an excellent spot for fall fishing under the ice, situated on the Kellett River, the famous river which after many bends and falls, flows into Pelly Bay and gives the best char of the whole Arctic. Doug Wilkinson back at Pelly Bay accompanied Father but again became ill and returned South, to be replaced by Ken Campbell as photographer. A cameraman's lot, specially in the Arctic, is often far from being pleasant. Working outside, barehanded, Father Rousselière's fingers became swollen with rhumatism.

At the beginning of November, the team was at *Areak* or Simpson Lake, a lake 30 kilometres long, filming winter scenes. On November 9, the task accomplished, they broke camp and headed for Pelly Bay. The skidoo driven by Father Mary-Rousselière left about 10:00 a.m., towing a sled heavily loaded with the camping paraphernalia on top of which Ken Campbell held his balance. Bernard and his dogs followed at a slower pace. Father Mary was driving at a good speed in order to put behind him as quickly as possible the bad sea ice. Visibility was poor with no perspective or shadow to indicate the relief or the contours of the terrain. About ten kilometres after leaving the camp, he crossed a snow covered plateau full of protruding long grass which at a given point parted as if to border an all white route which in reality was only a ledge of hardened snow jutting out in the emptiness. Almost immediately and without warning, the skidoo plunged into a ravine many metres deep that the driver had no time to avoid, followed inevitably by the sled and its passenger. Ken picked himself up in soft snow, happily with no damage, while Father Rousselière, half ejected from his vehicle found himself face first in the snow and in a piteous state, with his shoulder and right arm injured. He was visibly in great pain but managed to sit on the skidoo that had bravely endured the impact. Ken made a shoulder sling with a piece of the canvas that covered the sled and tried to immobilize as best he could Father Rousselière's right arm without knowing exactly the gravity of the injury. In the beginning Father could move his right hand and fingers but little by little all sensation disappeared.

Bernard who knew the area well—and its bad spots—arrived about an hour after the accident. He helped Father to get up and to climb the other side of the ravine. Then he made the Father a bed of skins on the sled, and drove him to Paul Kutsiutikku's camp near the Dew Line at *Atanaslerk*. Ken was amazed to witness the attention that Paul and Bernard lavished on Ataata Mari. They sat him on a caribou skin, then slipped him into the interior of the igloo and gave him a bit of boiled fish to eat. Ken wrote a note addressed to the Dew Line, explaining the situation and asking for help. Bernard took the note and walking as rapidly as he could in the soft snow, after four hours, delivered it to the station chief. Immediately the latter sent a snowmobile with a crew used to emergencies and trained to give first aid care. They bandaged the Father expertly, placed him delicately on a stretcher and travelling slowly to avoid the snow bumps, arrived at the Dew Line site about 2:00 a.m. All the way, in spite of his discomfort, Father Rousselière never complained. A plane was immediately chartered but the fog rose and prevented it from landing. Finally, on November 12, Father arrived at Foxe Main where the doctor diagnosed a fracture of the dislocated shoulder. He succeeded putting everything back in place but unfortunately the nerves had been damaged and he deemed evacuation necessary. The next day, an RCAF Albatross took him to Winnipeg and for two months, he was treated at the Saint Boniface Hospital.

The news of the accident spread all over Canada and France like moss fire in the tundra, although not causing as much sensation as the assassination of President John Kennedy. The convalescence augured to be long.

On January 7, 1964, Father Rousselière was accepted at the Rehabilitation Institute of Montreal. In March, he became an outpatient and took a room at the Provincial house of the Oblates on *Avenue du Musée*. He had to go daily for physiotherapy treatments to make the articulation of his right hand more supple. He also practised writing with his left hand anxious at least to be able to sign his name. The impossibility to celebrate Mass was his greatest sorrow. He wanted to offer the Holy Sacrifice for his dear mother whose death was announced to him on February 16, 1964. He swallowed his sadness and having to stay in Montreal, he registered anew at the University and wrote his thesis for a master's degree in Anthropology, typewriting his texts, slowly, with one finger of his left hand. All the time, he kept his optimism and never doubted that he would get well again. Indeed, gradually, he recovered partial use of his right hand and in September was finally able to celebrate Mass again and write short letters. The progress he made was so impressive that the doctors who treated him would find it nothing less than miraculous.

Pond Inlet—Pelly Bay—Pontoise

Meanwhile, the Pond Inlet mission was not totally abandoned. Father Lorson coming from Gjoa Haven stayed there from February to April 1964. Terry Ryan, artistic counsellor of the Cape Dorset Co-operative, on an informatory tour of the North, resided there for several weeks. Finally, Father Rousselière felt well enough to go back north. He arrived at Mittimatalik on February 4, 1965, on board the DC 3 that from Iqaluit flew from settlement to settlement picking up the teachers of different localities for a conference in Yellowknife. On February 15, the new Canadian flag with the maple leaf was officially inaugurated. At the request of the administrator, Bill Berry, Father translated the Queen's proclamation from English to Inuktitut and the Anglican Minister said an appropriate prayer in front of the natives surrounding the new national emblem. It was bitterly cold.

On March 13, boarding an R.C.M.P. plane passing through Pond Inlet on its way to Cambridge Bay, he landed at Pelly Bay. Father Vandevelde was not there to greet him, still in the hospital at St. Boniface since the previous October. He needed a long rest that was crowned by a stay in Belgium allowing him to celebrate Christmas with his own people. Father Lorson then in Igloolik came to temporarily replace Father Vandevelde in Pelly Bay, caring for the Inuit, victims of an intestinal flu; warning them against the danger of catching rabies from the foxes coming near the igloos; searching for an exterior market for the Eskimo sculptures made of ivory and caribou antler, real master-pieces admired by the white people visiting Pelly. Father Lorson also wondered how he could adapt the new rules concerning the liturgy of the mass to the local celebrations in vernacular.

Bob Young, the excellent cameraman who had won first prize in Venice, continued to film the Eskimo life in winter camps with Ataata Mari, Asen Balikci and Ken Post. They lived in an igloo. On the first day of hunting, at the breathing hole, luck was with them. After waiting an hour and a half, immobile, bent in two, Zacharie saw the little ball of fur he had delicately placed on top of the hole starting to move, signalling the approach of a seal and sure of his movement, he harpooned it.

At the end of the filming, Father Mary-Rousselière was convinced that the ultimate documentary film on the Eskimo had been shot. Everything had been filmed, whether it was dancing to the sound of the drums, games of strength, meals prepared by the women or other scenes depicting the lives and culture of Inuit.

On March 20, Pelly Bay welcomed Bishop Lacroix who came to give the sacrament of confirmation to young Inuit. Wrapped in his black cassock and wearing seal skin boots, Father Rousselière became once more the simple priest happy to hear confessions or to listen to the Bishop giving the latest news concerning the Vicariate. On April 6, the Apostolic Pronuncio of Canada, His Excellency Bishop Sergio Pignedoli stopped at Pelly Bay during his visit to the Arctic missions. He was delighted to learn more about the Inuit and their land and to photograph the first igloo he had ever seen. He would also witness the northern invasion of southern civilization, hearing the noise of the tractors building a runway long enough to accommodate *Nordair's* DC6, due soon to bring the settlement's supplies. He publicly praised Fathers Lorson and Rousselière for their devotion to the cause of the Inuit.

At the end of April 1965, when he was in Montreal, Father Mary met Monseigneur Clabaut. The Bishop was on his way to Hall Beach where he had been called to preach the retreat for the Oblates of the northern zone. Regretfully, Father Rousselière was unable to participate in the retreat as he arrived at Sanerajak only on June 1, anxious to go back to Pond Inlet and to resume his archaeological excavations.

On the 24, he made a reconnaissance trip to the Eskimo camps, at *Igluluarjuit, Qinnibvik* and *Arnaviapik*. He found all the families well provided with caribou meat.

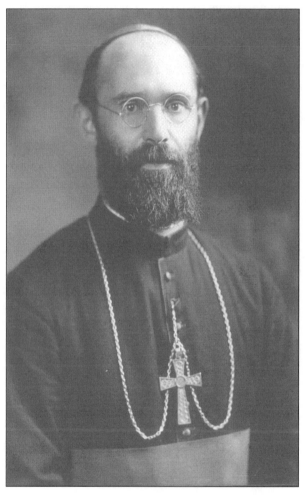

Bishop Clabaut

After *Kanayortuq*, the ice became so bad that it was impossible to continue by dog sled without danger; at the entrance of Tay Sound, he crashed through the ice and took a very cold bath! All the miseries of the trip were soon forgotten when he discovered an authentic pre-Dorset site nearby in a spot called *Eqaluit.* Mid-July, there was finally enough open water to allow Ataata Mari to explore the coast.

When he returned to Pond Inlet on August 7, the *C. D. Howe* was anchored in the bay. Thanks to Captain Lavoie's kindness, he flew by helicopter over the peak of *Qurvinaluk,* without much success as the ground was still covered with snow. Never forgetting that he was primarily a priest, he celebrated Sunday Mass on the boat for the members of the crew who wished to attend.

A few days later, he made an historical find when he located the tomb of *Mittima.* Pond Inlet, as noted before, is called *Mittimatalik* in Inuktitut, that is the place of Mittamatalik's tomb, a famous Inuk who died more than 200 years ago and was probably a relative of the Greenlandic Eskimos. Father Danielo would probably have thrown some light on the question if the Lord had not called him back to Him on October 8, 1965. Hoping that one day he would be sent as a missionary in Greenland, he had read and studied intensively the ancient history of this mysterious and attractive country.

From September 9 to 16, Father Rousselière went to *Nadlua*, then to *Nunguvik* in Navy Board Inlet to continue his digging until the ground froze, rendering all efforts useless. From there he witnessed the migration of the narwhals that were leaving North before winter.

At Christmas, many Inuit attended Midnight Mass. At the meal following the service, Father offered them a cup of salted tea, maybe the most appalling drink in the

Guy Mary-Rousselière excavating at Nunguvik

world! He had collected ice close to the iceberg and sincerely thought it was unsalted ice. The Inuit did not react immediately but a few days later Panikpakutsuk brought him a load of good unsalted ice and Father understood! A story without words: Anyone who wishes to be an Inuk does not necessarily become one!

To mark the beginning of 1966, there was nothing special except the usual blowing snow, the wedding of two Whites in the Anglican church, the capturing by Maktar of a shark that would be sent to Italy, and, in March, the arrival of the plane that took Father Rousselière to Chesterfield Inlet where most of the Oblates were assembled to participate in the retreat preached by Monseigneur Leguerrier, the Bishop of James Bay. Bishop Leguerrier had been present at the Vatican II Council and gave interesting comments on the sessions. The liturgy in Inuktitut was the origin of many useful discussions among the missionaries who more or less were all fluent in the native tongue.

After a short stay at Pelly Bay where Father became very ill with the flu, he travelled to Montreal and to France. He left Pontoise at the beginning of August after visiting his family and meeting the archaeologists interested in his Arctic excavations. Always absent-minded, it was not unusual for him to forget things here and there or to take small objects which did not belong to him. One day, in Paris, he went to the train station, suitcases in hand, and walked to the ticket office. He put his luggage on the floor, asked for a ticket, paid for it and, retrieving his suitcases, proceeded to the quay where he had to board the train. He had the strange feeling that someone was following him. Turning abruptly around, he said to the stranger: "What's the matter, Sir?" And the stranger answered him: "Nothing,

Sir, but I would appreciate if you would give me back my suitcase, the one you are carrying!"

On August 20, 1966, he returned North in the company of the Honourable Arthur Laing, Minister of Northern Affairs and Natural Resources, travelling with members of the Economic Council of Canada, who were greatly interested in the exploitation of the mines discovered in the northern part of Baffin Land. After a stopover first at Mary River, then at Milne Inlet, the bad weather prevented the party to continue to Resolute Bay and, instead, they landed in Hall Beach where Father Rousselière left the Minister's company and waited for the regular Nordair flight going to Resolute Bay. At Resolute, he stayed a few days aboard the *McLean*; then, he transferred to another government ice breaker, the *MacDonald*, under the leadership of Captain Fournier, leaving for Milne Inlet. From there, he completed the last forty miles to Pond Inlet aboard the ship's helicopter.

A few days later the *McLean* arrived with the wood necessary to build 25 small Eskimo houses and the supplies for the mission. Father Rousselière also received a more powerful radio transmitter which would allow him to establish contact with the other Hudson Bay missions and even with Father Lynge at the time posted in Greenland. Taking advantage of the last days of summer and with Uqalik's help, he built a small wooden shed close to the mission in order to replace the former hangar which was covered with sheets of rusty metal.

In September 1966, the Revue "*Cahiers de Géographie du Québec*" published a long article written by Father Guy Mary-Rousselière entitled "*Toponymie Esquimaude de la Région de Pond Inlet*" (Eskimo Toponymy of the Pond Inlet Region) accompanied by a map on which were situated the different areas mentioned in the text; it also gave a list of 245 inuktitut words and their meanings. Analyzing the names of the different places, he divided them into four categories, according to the geographic origin, the physical characteristics of the land, the particularities of certain areas and finally the Eskimo customs.

The erudite article began like this: "The Pond Inlet Eskimos, known also as Tununirmiut (singular: Tununirmiutak) belong to what Rasmussen called the Igloolik Eskimo, a group which also embraced the Admiralty Inlet Tununirusirmiut, the Igluligmiut of Igloolik and the Aiviligmiut of Republse Bay. In language and customs, they are also very near the Akudnirmiut of Clyde River." This short extract is sufficient to give you the tone of Father Mary's writing. This is not a child's fairy tale but the work of an expert in ethnology, an expert who speaks the language of the country very well and has taken the time to consult the elders and is determined to go as deep as possible in the subject.

On October 14, he left Pond Inlet again and went to Montreal for minor surgery. He also visited the National Film Board and finally on December 5, 1966, accompanied by Ken Post and Jacques Drouin, N.F.B. technicians, he reached Pelly Bay with the special mission of recording the sound for the ethnographic films on the *Nitjilit* Inuit. At Christmas, Father concelebrated Midnight Mass with Father André Goussaert who was then in charge of the mission of Pelly Bay and was also an ardent promoter of the Arctic Co-operative Movement. Both priests shared the popular dinner with the Inuit and all enjoyed the buns baked by Brother Vermersch, o.m.i.. The next day, a beautiful winter day, about 20 dog teams gathered on the sea for the customary race, bringing joy to the whole population and prizes to a few winners.

On February 27, 1967, Father was back at Pond Inlet. The village was becoming more and more modernized. It now had a radio station broadcasting one hour every day. Father had been elected as a member of the committee responsible for the radio programs, not a very important job but still a proof that the people of Pond Inlet knew of his desire to work towards their welfare and the development of the settlement. Everyone was welcome at the mission. It was open to anyone from far and near who knocked at the door. He lodged a young student in anthropology, Jerôme Rousseau; he gave shelter to some Americans from the New York Aquarium who came to study the possibility of catching live narwhals. On June 7, in a sentence as brief as the Episcopal visit itself, he noted that Monseigneur Lacroix had come to perform the confirmations and had stayed but four hours! On the other hand, two days later, Father Maurice Métayer, missionary in the Mackenzie diocese and a good friend, came to visit him and stayed two weeks. They went together to Button Point to continue archaeological excavations. All the time they were there, they dig and dig, slowly, patiently, following the regression of the permafrost until the day when Father Métayer had to go home. From July 17 to August 28, Father Mary was at *Nunguvik*, a place with a curse. According to the legend, an old woman, her face hidden behind a mask, frightened to death all the inhabitants of the camp in order to take revenge for the mistreatment doled out to her grandson. From *Nunguvik,* when he was not looking for artifacts, Father could see numerous narwhals swimming along the coast. On September 8, from *Saatut* where he had moved by boat, Alain brought him back to Pond Inlet, the meteorological conditions being far from favourable to keep on excavating. A terrible storm had even torn the roof off his tent. At the post, huge waves had eroded the coast making the habitual landing wharf unfit for use.

Nevertheless, he succeeded placing on board the *Iberville* many cases containing archaeological specimens for delivery to the National Museum in Ottawa.

In fall, Father Mary went to Montreal and returned to Pond early December. On the 23rd, in his small chapel, he blessed the marriage of Leigh Brintnell a white teacher, with Bernadette Tagak, a young Inuk girl, the sister of Maktar.

Father Mary-Rousselière's reputation as a great scholar and a gentleman was spreading and in spite of his timidity, because of his charming personality, he was contracting long-lasting friendships. Ken Post, one of the film producers of the Pelly Bay team mentioned earlier, called from Resolute to ask him for two Eskimo husky dogs. Ken was at the time the cameraman of an expedition en route to the North Pole, an expedition which according to Father Rousselière's prediction was doomed to failure by lack of experience and the absence of good dog teams. His prediction was confirmed in February when the disappointed travellers turned around after having covered only a few miles on the ice north of Alert.

11

CHESTERFIELD, FRANCE, GREENLAND

At Chesterfield, at the end of April, Father Mary-Rousselière with some fellow Oblates took part in the annual retreat preached by Father Marcel Gilbert, a veteran of the Oblate Scholasticate of Ottawa. On this occasion, they celebrated the silver anniversary of Monseigneur Lacroix as Bishop of the Hudson Bay Diocese. Worn out by travel, the worries of a vast territory and sickness, the Bishop was soon to resign. The religious jubilee of Father Ducharme, the veteran of Arviat and the 25th sacerdotal anniversary of Father René Belair, the diocesan bursar, were also commemorated. During the study sessions, questions concerning the catechists, the cooperatives, the liturgy in the Inuktitut language and the relations between Catholic, Anglican and Moravian Churches, were brought to the attention of the participants. All these matters were of prime importance in the evangelization of the the Canadian Arctic Inuit.

Father Rousselière then spent the summer in France, visiting his family, the Museum of Man, his fellow Oblates and old friends of his younger years. Then he left en route for Greenland. August 6, 1968, he took the plane at Orly for Copenhagen where he met his friend

Jørgen Meldgaard. He presented his film *Lux in Tenebris* at the Danish National Museum. Kaj Birket-Smith, renowned ethnologist, last survivor of the 5th Thule expedition, recognized the Eskimos as he had known them in 1923!

Then it was Iceland with a change of planes at Keflavik. From there, in less than four hours flying, he went to Narssarsuaq, south of Greenland, landing on an old runway built by the Americans during the war. Now by helicopter, now by boat, he visited the West Coast of the Island. At Godthab (Nuuk), he received a warm welcome from the Governor of Greenland, Mr. Christensen, and, the following day, he was a guest of honor at a reception organized in honour of the King and Queen of Denmark of which Greenland is a part. Then, as guest of the three Oblate Fathers who represented the Catholic Church in the country, ministering to about twenty followers under their wings, he got acquainted with the diverse aspects of the Greenlandic civilization, its bilingualism, its literature, its raising of sheep and reindeer, its fishing, its whale hunting and evidently, its monuments and ruins, vestiges of the Vikings and remains of the medieval Catholicity. He regretted that the co-operative movement was not yet rooted among the *Kalâtdlit*, the Greenlandic Eskimos, and that the scourges of civilization had been introduced there, such as alcoholism and birth control. At Frederikshaab, he visited a small coquettish Lutheran Church with red walls and a green roof. And finally, the 21st of August, from *Narssarsuaq*, he flew via Iceland towards Canada and arrived at Pond Inlet at the beginning of September 1968.

At Quebec, in February 1969, he visited at the hospital for the war veterans, Alfred Tremblay, a former prospector who in 1910-1911 had spent the winter in the Arctic with Bernier and who, in 1912, was the first white man to cross Baffin Land in the company of an Eskimo family.

The trip lasted a year and was so hard that Captain Bernier thought Tremblay had died. Alfred Tremblay is the author of the book *"The Cruise of the Minnie Maud"*. That year three boats had gone in search of gold at Pond Inlet, without success. One even was crushed by the ice and sank. When Tremblay heard that Father Mary-Rousselière was coming from Pond Inlet, he cried for joy and kept him for dinner.

Father was planning another trip to Greenland but this time in the region of Thule. In order to prepare this new expedition, he went to Yellowknife, the capital of the North, to meet the Commissioner and explain his project for 1970, the centennial year of the Northwest Territories. He was promised a $2,000.00 grant to defray, in part, the trip to Greenland, but with strings attached. The participants had to include some Inuit of Pond Inlet, some of Arctic Bay and some of Resolute Bay and they had to travel either by dogsled or by skidoo. "Evidently", wrote Father Rousselière, "the people of Yellowknife do not have the least idea what such a trip can represent. The eastern part of Lancaster Sound rarely freezes over and we would be obliged to go very far west to be able to go across. By skidoo, it would be a risk. And the trip back and forth by dogsled would take at a minimum, five months; this would mean that we would have to return by boat. The migrants of the last century took five years to make the trip". The governmental authorities had to accept the fact that they had in Father Mary-Rousselière an expert in Eskimology, always ready to dig not only the ground but the history of the Inuit. His article on the *"Eskimo Toponymy of the Pond Inlet Region"* published by "Les Éditions de l'Université Laval" at Québec had drawn the attention of the specialists of the Arctic but, as for the politicians, it did not seem to have touched the right chord.

New excavations at Pond Inlet

Due to a grant from the Canada Arts Council, Father
Rousselière bought a plane ticket to Pond Inlet for Bernard
Vezin, a young Frenchman originally from Savoy, professor of Physical Education at the Stanislaus College in
Montreal. Bernard landed at Pond on July 12, 1969, and
two days later, left for *Nunguvik* by dogsled with his mentor. The season was already advanced, pools of deep water
forming on the surface of the ice; cracks sometimes so wide
that to cross over, they had to use pieces of ice as rafts.
Once or twice, they took an unexpected bath in the icy
water but luckily without any ill effects. At *Nunguvik*,
Father and his companion felt more isolated than the
American astronauts presently on the moon. The digging
had barely begun when Bernard had an acute bout of
tendinitis. Fearing that his co-worker would have a recur-
rence of the crisis that had partially paralysed him three
years earlier, Father Mary judged that evacuation was
necessary. Alas! his small transmitter could not reach
anyone. So with whale bones he wrote on the ground the
word "*SICK*" and it was just mere luck that the next day the
twin Otter of Atlas Aviation flew over to drop mail. The
pilot, Dick de Blicquy, having seen the S.O.S. sign, landed
on a small sandy beach about three kilometres from the camp
and took Bernard Vezin back with him to the south. Left
alone with Arnakadlak, Ataata Mari continued his research
and having discovered a new site near *Nunguvik*, he gave
it the name of his helper, the *Arnakadlak* Site. Another
Inuk, Asamik, came to get him by canoe for a quick
exploration of Milne Inlet with a stopover at *Qurlurtuq,*
near a waterfall impressive, not for its height, but its
considerable amount of water. Downstream, one could
see fish resting before jumping the falls. According to the

Nutarak, Qaunak and Ataata Mari at Amakadlak

biologists of the Wildlife Services, it may be one of the most important locations in the entire North for the movement of Arctic char. Boiled, fried or frozen, the char is delicious. What could be better as an entrée to a banquet of fresh caribou meat!

At the end of August 1969, alerted by a few silex points that the children had brought him, he started to dig in the middle of the Pond Inlet settlement and discovered two magnificent pre-Dorset harpoon heads dating back 2435 years B.C. Just a charming anecdote: Susan, the young nine year old daughter of the new administrator, John Scullion, and her little friend, came to ask Father Mary if they could help him, and permission being granted, they returned immediately with small spoons and forks to take part in the research!

While Father was discovering these vestiges of a past civilization, comfortable low-cost rental housing was being built for the Mittimataligmiut, with all the utilities included in the very low rental price. There was also free access to the dispensary where dedicated and qualified nurses were welcoming the sick, the pregnant women or the victims of accident. As for the boys and girls, the day school was still in operation, giving them elementary education and lunch without, however, assuring them of a job after their graduation.

At Christmas the mission was almost bursting at the seams for Midnight Mass, there were more Protestants than Catholics attending! In May 1970, when Monseigneur Emmanuel Clarizio, Apostolic Pronuncio in Canada, accompanied by Father Yvon Levaque, o.m.i., Director of the Indianescom in Ottawa, visited Pond Inlet, he was amazed to see so many scholarly books in the missionary's library. The modest size of the priest's residence recalled to his mind the small house of the

Holy Family in Nazareth. In his opinion, if Christ was to return to earth, it would no doubt be at Pond Inlet for he would find there the real poverty of the first missionary era. It was perhaps this same conclusion that was shared by Leif Zeillich-Jansen, a very friendly and convinced Christian, Professor of History at Stockholm University, who spent a few months at Pond Inlet to study the traditional Eskimo religious beliefs.

Equally in May 1970, Father Rousselière was visited by the editor of the *National Geographic Magazine* from Washington, a visit that resulted in the publication of 30 pages of text and marvelous Inuit photographs in the February 1971 issue, a real treat to look at and to read. It is all about the ancestral life of the Inuk from the day he rested as a baby on his mother's back, up to the grave made of rocks that will shelter the last remains of the old man. Photographs catch light and shadow in an igloo illuminated by the seal oil lamp. Regarding his study of the Inuit, Father Mary writes: "I have always sought out the Eskimos in their igloos to learn their ways, approaching them not only as priest, but as hunting companion, an amateur doctor, and as anthropologist. I have been their teacher and they have been mine. Often I have felt that I understood them well. But then, always, some small incident will convince me that I still have much to learn."

Again during the first days of May 1970, Ron Sheardon, the pilot of Murray Watts (the discoverer of the famous bed of iron at Mary River) landed as usual at Pond Inlet and invited a few friends, among whom was Father Rousselière, to fly over the *S.S. Manhattan* in Lancaster Sound. The gigantic ice breaker, the largest oil tanker of the American Merchant fleet, had, from September to November 1969, crossed in both directions the famous Northwest Passage as far as Barrow Point, bringing back from Prudhoe Bay as a souvenir of this historical feat, a barrel of oil. At the end of the same month May 1970, at a time when the ice was still thick and solid, the *S. S. Manhattan* was at the entrance of Pond Inlet. Father went to dinner at the invitation of the Captain and travelled there by snowmobile.The latter assured him that in a few years more powerful icebreakers would all winter long be able to evacuate the ore mined in the North. Father was not completely convinced of this, because the *Manhattan* and the *Saint Laurent* (a Canadian icebreaker that accompanied the giant ship) had already encountered difficulty making headway through the polar ice.

In June, writing to Monseigneur Omer Robidoux[1], a native of Saint-Pierre-Jolys, Manitoba, recently appointed Bishop of the Churchill-Hudson Bay Diocese, he congratulated him on his recent ordination and invited him to come and see for himself the situation of the Catholic Mission at Pond Inlet. Father Mary told him he blessed the union of two Eskimos, the first native marriage in the annals of the Mission! He also did not lose any time expressing his concern about the future of the *Eskimo* magazine. The great majority of Inuit had abandoned their traditional way of life, the very life that mainly interested the general public. They are now living more and more as the *Qallunaat*, the white men, imitating them in many ways, although fundamentally, they had remained true to their culture.

Tragic events brought him enough material to fill the magazine with unexpected articles. For example, a fire destroyed, on November 26, 1969, the mission-chapel of Repulse Bay built only three years before. Father Didier, in

---

[1] Omer Robidoux, born at St. Pierre, Manitoba, November 19, 1913, Oblate missionary among the Indians, principal of Indian schools at Lestock, Lebret, Winnipeg, ordained Bishop of Churchill-Hudson Bay, May 21,1970, by Cardinal Flahiff, deceased in a plane accident at Rankin Inlet, N.W.T., November 12, 1986.

Eskimo Vol. 83 Spring-Summer 1970, described the disaster. He told the readers how the smoke, then the flames under the furnace fanned by a violent wind soon caused a general conflagration. Nothing could be saved except a few translations and the Tabernacle, containing the Consecrated Host. Father Joannes Rivoire[2], on his return from France, found only ashes.

Another tragedy worse than a fire was written by Father Fournier in a moving article entitled: *An Eskimo Leader, Pacôme Qulaut*. Qulaut, an Inuk from Igloolik was driving back for the benefit of the local Coop a tractor that had been saved from the dump on the Dew Line when he broke through the sea ice and drowned. Father Rousselière expressed his condolences on the occasion of Pacôme's disappearance and felt his duty to render him homage, as he had often travelled with him in the past. He had on several occasions appreciated his intelligence, his desire to improve himself, his resourcefulness, his dedication, and at the same time, a rarer thing, his personal commitment towards his religion. An American anthropologist said about Qulaut: "The death of any man impoverishes the world but, with Qulaut, it is an exceptional being that disappears from among us."

The same could have been said about Jean Ayaruar who died in Rankin Inlet at the age of 62. Father Ducharme who knew him well gave a condensed version of his life in *Eskimo* Vol.84, Fall-Winter 1970. Son of a sorcerer, full blooded Inuk, good hunter, baptized by Monseigneur Turquetil in 1917, travelling companion to the missionaries, one of the three Eskimos who in 1938 went to the Eucharistic Congress in Quebec, struck by tuberculosis at

---

[2] Joannès Rivoire, French Oblate born in 1931. In the Inuit missions from 1960 to 1993.

age 42, then more or less cured but weakened in body but not in spirit, he accompanied and advised the Inuit in their evolution to a more modern life. Ayaruar wrote his autobiography in syllabic characters, a publication financed by the Ministry of Northern Affairs, as reported in a note added to the article by Father Rousselière who knew him well and was aware of the esteem that was his, from Repulse to Arviat.

To pull *Eskimo* out of a financial deficit, Father Mary who remained the editor responsible of the magazine, proposed to readers a one dollar subscription, barely enough even then to cover the mailing expenses but at least a silent invitation to good-hearted subscribers to show according to their means their generosity for the missionary cause.

In July, it was again time to think of excavating. Thanks to a biologist who had a plane at his disposal, Father took aerial photographs of the main sites. One day, the administrator John Scullion brought him a wooden mask painted in red ochre that had been discovered by Joshua Inuksuk at Button Point, an authentic specimen of the Dorset culture, at least a thousand years old. He sent it immediately to the Director of the National Museum in Ottawa. An American tourist, Mr. Ash, offered to fly Father Mary and Colly Scullion to the spot where the mask had been found. They accepted gratefully and, very much in luck, in a few hours, they unearthed two drum frames and many small wooden figurines.

Another expedition by canoe at the end of August in Milne Inlet by rain and melting snow brought nothing sensational except a dive when Father slipped on the edge of the boat and fell on his back in to the water. Reaching the shore, he removed his trousers, changed his underwear and borrowed a pair of pants from an Inuk.

And while the polar night again enveloped the region, Father Rousselière began to write long scholarly reports on

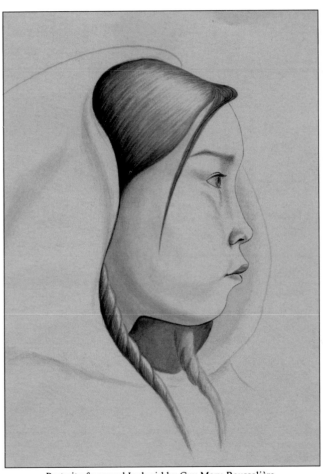
Portrait of a yound Inuk girl by Guy Mary-Rousselière

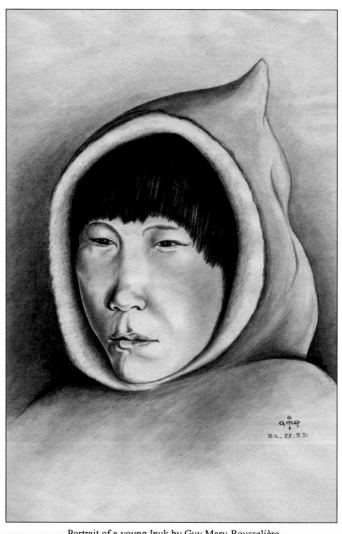

Portrait of a young Inuk by Guy Mary-Rousselière
(Baker Lake, March 1951)
Eskimo, Vol. 25, January 1952

Portrait of Okkomaluk by Guy Mary-Rousselière.
Eskimo, Vol. 38, December 1955

Portrait of Ludger Otak by Guy Mary-Rousselière.
Eskimo, Vol. 35, March 1955

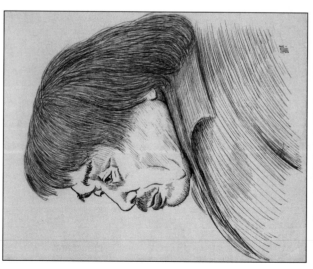

Portrait of Utukutsuk (Okakytyuk) by
Guy Mary-Rousselière.
Eskimo, Vol. 42, December 1956

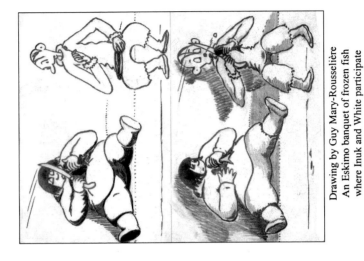

Portrait of Margarita Suna with her baby
by Guy Mary-Rousselière (Pingerkalik 1946).
Eskimo, Vol. 7, December 1947

Drawing by Guy Mary-Rousselière
An Eskimo banquet of frozen fish
where Inuk and White participate

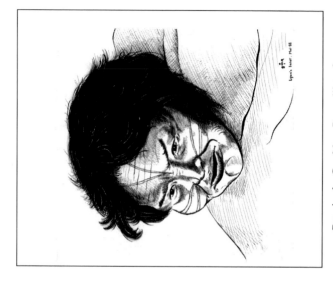

Drawing by Guy Mary-Rousselière of a
Tattooed Lady (Lyon's Inlet, May 1952)
Eskimo, Vol. 32, June 1954

Drawing of an Inuk smoking the pipe by
Guy Mary-Rousselière.
Eskimo, Vol. 10, September 1948

Drawing of a little Inuk boy
by Guy Mary-Rousselière (Siorardjuk, April 3, 1948).
Eskimo, Vol. 13, January 1949

Drawing by Guy Mary-Rousselière.
Young Inuk in caribou skin trousers and sealskin boots.

Drawing by Guy Mary-Rousselière illustrating the article *Mass In An Igloo* by
Father Etienne Danielo. *Eskimo, Vol. 35, March 1955*

Guy Mary-Rousselière and John Scullion with young son Christopher

his summer work and his discoveries at Button Point, not neglecting however other questions of great importance to him such as the Eskimo orthography. He never feared to voice his disagreement with the Gagné system adopted by Father Didier. He considered Father Schneider's dictionary the best of its kind. As for the new hymns to be sung in church, "give us," he said, "the melody with real notes, not caribou droppings coming down a stairwell!"

At Christmas 1970, he was happy to send as a gift to his Bishop a substantial cheque that he had earned by his talents as photographer and writer. He had still enough money left to pay for his coming trip to the South. The doctor who had examined him on the boat during the summer had found him in good health, but had however advised him as a measure of prudence since he was approaching the 60's, to consult an urologist. His legs were as good as new. He realized it when in fall near the Salmon River, he suddenly saw two bears coming towards him. Instantly, he recovered his twenty year old legs and ran as fast as he could to give the alarm in the settlement. As a matter of fact, they were just two hungry little cubs who were attracted by the scent of narwhals killed the night before. At the sight of Father Mary, they ran back to the sea. Boats were put in the water and the chase started. After some considerable time, both cubs were lassoed by the Inuit, put in crates and brought to shore in front of an enthusiastic audience of women and children. Of course, the little bears were not pleased to be in captivity and were fighting to escape. They were hungry. The children led by Susan Scullion decided that they needed honey sandwiches. To make the cubs calmer, the nurse put some tranquilizers in the sandwiches but they spat them out. The next step was to put the pills in some fresh *maktaq* (whale blubber) and that was immediately swallowed and the young bears eventually were more relaxed. A few days later, duly sedated, they were put on a plane and sent to a zoo in the south. They are probably now still entertaining millions of visitors!

Montreal—Ottawa—Chesterfield—Pond Inlet

In February 1971, Father Mary went to Montreal, and found himself in the middle of a snowstorm, with all traffic at a standstill. Later in Ottawa, as was usual on all his visits in the Capital, he spent long hours at the Museum studying, analysing or photographing specimens and meeting officials in charge of the preservation of artifacts. He always wore a grey or black suit and his Roman collar that identified him as a priest. One day, on the bus, alone with the driver, the latter asked him to hear his confession: "Bless me, Father.." and thus it was done between Argyle and the Bus Terminal. Father Rousselière did not approve of priests dressed in bright colours or having long hair falling on their shoulders, no more than he approved of Sisters in miniskirts. Once when he was in Washington, he saw the Little Sisters of Jesus in their long dresses and on their chest, a large cross. He was pleased and convinced that their habit did not at all diminish their profound influence on the black milieu where they exercised their ministry.

In March 1971, he attended the Oblate's retreat at Chesterfield Inlet. It was preached by Father Joseph Meeùs[3], a Belgian Oblate whose spirituality was simple and vibrant as the chords of his guitar. He also was present when the Consul General of France at Edmonton, Mr. Raymond Huleu, presented the medal of the "Chevalier de l'Ordre National du Mérite" to Father Pierre Henry, the Apostle of

[3] Joseph Meeùs, born in Belgium in 1927. Oblate missionary, after working in the Labrador-Schefferville Diocese until 1968, came to the Inuit missions of the Hudson Bay Diocese and is now in charge of Igloolik and Superior of the Hudson Bay Delegation.

the *Nitjilit,* better known in the North under the name of *Kayualuk* or Red Beard, as explained previously.

On March 26, a small plane, an *Aztec* brought him back to Pond inlet via Repulse Bay where he stopped just long enough to see the improvements brought to living conditions of Inuit and the influence of the co-operative movement on the welfare of the people. Bishop Robidoux accompanied him to Pond Inlet but, unfortunately, stayed only two hours, exactly the time that the pilot allowed him before flying back to Churchill.

A grant from the Canada Arts Council subsidized his summer excavation at Button Point in the company of the Scullion family and two remarkable visitors, Sheila Burnford and Susan Ross. Author of great renown,— she wrote *The Incredible Journey*—Sheila Burnford will give her impressions on the country, its inhabitants and on Father Mary himself, in a very interesting book entitled: *One Woman's Arctic.* Susan Ross, an artist, the niece of the great film producer Flaherty, is well known to the readers of *Eskimo* for her beautiful drawings. A photographer, Eberhart Otto, of *Arts Canada* magazine joined the excavators. Not only the trip by dogsled but also the archaeological discoveries were interesting, composed of important mask fragments, wooden artifacts, etc. Later, while digging in the Dorset ruins at *Nunguvik*, he was helped by Richard Geurts, a 17 year old university student, the nephew of the famous pilot of Arctic Wings, Charley Weber. Dick de Blicquy, another ace of the northern aviation, landed them near the site in a Twin Otter, a plane which did not need a long runway. When eight days later, *Juupi* and *Nutarak* joined them by dogsled and canoe, Ataata Mari entrusted them with the task of digging the Thule houses, of course under his own supervision. He also experimented with them a replica of a pre-Dorset harpoon

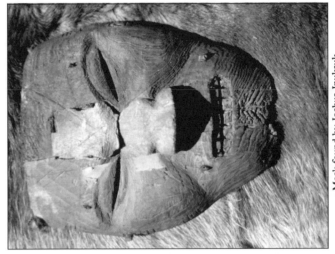

Mask found by Joshua Inuksuk
at Button Point (June 1971)

Nutarak

197

made of caribou antler and was amazed to find it so effective not only to hunt seals but even narwhals. "In my opinion," he wrote, "more than 4,000 years ago, the ideal form of the harpoon had already been found".

During excavations at *Nunguvik*, in Navy Board Inlet, he had the good fortune of discovering, in a Dorset habitation of the seventh century, small wooden lathes that according to him could come only from one or several reduced models of flat bottom covered crafts. Were these miniatures mere toys, funereal ornaments or objects used in certain religious ceremonies? He would not commit himself but found at the site proof that the Dorset people were well equipped to travel by sea and to hunt sea mammals in open water during the summer. The remains of whalebones found in the ruins of their dwellings corroborated his opinion. (Cf. *Eskimo N.S.,* N° 3, Spring-Summer *1972)*.

In October 1971, the Bell Company came north to repair telephone lines and install them on posts. Short and long distance communications were established. Unfortunately, news passed on by phone was not always good. In March, on the shore, a woman was found frozen, victim of alcohol. And now, in December, at Iqaluit, an Inuk under the influence of liquor, had assassinated his son with an axe. The murderer was well known, having lived formerly at Mittimatalik and being a former parishioner of the Catholic mission. Evidently the temptation to get intoxicated was very strong for the Inuit, especially for those who worked for the government or mining companies and drew good salaries. At Christmas, such an individual, dead-drunk, entered the church during Midnight Mass and caused some disturbance. Father had to refuse him Holy Communion. "Too often", wrote Father Rousselière, "money brings with it only moral corruption."

Personally, at the end of his life, he would admit that he never had bought a bottle of alcoholic beverage, although faithful to his French origins, he knew how to appreciate a wine of good vintage! The Anglican Minister, the Reverend Howard Bracewell, was also worried because of the Inuit propensity to drink to excess. Howard was later sent to Quito, Ecuador where he preached in Inuktitut the virtues of sobriety through an evangelical radio station called the *"Voice of the Andes"*! He was replaced in Pond Inlet by the Reverend Laurie Dexter, who later reached the North Pole on skis.

The year 1971 ended rather coldly. One of the two generators furnishing electricity to the village exploded and the second undoubtedly in sympathy also stopped, leaving the houses without heat or light except for the police detachment that had its own generating set and generously opened its doors to the victims of the breakdown. Father Rousselière distributed candles as long as his supply lasted! Fortunately that same night, all was functioning again except some water pipes that were solidly frozen.

Greenland—Godthaad—cutting up a whale

The translation of Qillarsuaq—The Story of a Polar Migration
1. Hans Engelund Kristiansen
2. Arine Kristiansen—translator into Greenlandic
3. Guy Mary-Rouselière
4. Sophie Steltner—translator into German
5. Hermann Steltner—initiator of the project (Photo Kristiansen)

12

POLAR MIGRATION

Greenland

The year 1972 was for Father Mary-Rousselière, o.m.i., the year of long trips. Some who are of a facetious mind translate the initials "o.m.i." added to the names of the Oblates by *"Opera Mea Itinera"* which means roughly: "My occupation is to travel"! How true! First, in April, he went to Greenland, in the footsteps of Qitdlarssuaq[1], with some Inuit of Pond Inlet, Igloolik and Arctic Bay, a plane trip made possible with financial help from the Honourable Gerard Pelletier, Secretary of State, Mr Stuart Hodgson, Commissioner of the Northwest Territories and other official organizations. The object of the trip was to renew contacts between the two countries. Father Mary-Rousselière prolonged his stay in the region of Thule and collected information for the book published in 1980 by the Montreal University Press and entitled: *Qitdlarssuaq, the History of a Polar Migration.* Father Rousselière himself, suggested to some of his friends who wanted to know more on the migration, to read the story of this historic trip as told in detail in the *Eskimo* N.S. N°. 4,

---

[1] Spelled sometimes differently: Qidlarjuaq, Qitdlarssuaq, Kilarjuar, etc.

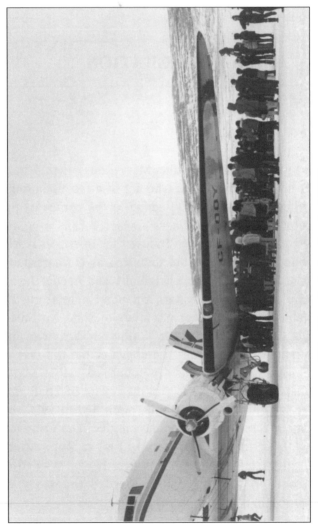

Visit of Canadian Inuit to Greenland (1972)
(Photo Hans Engelund Kristiansen)

Fall-Winter 1972. It is my pleasure to copy here extensive parts of that same article:

On the Footsteps of Qitdlarssuaq

As the Atlas-Aviation DC-3 lifted off the ice runway of Pond Inlet, early in the morning of April 7, 1972, and set its course towards Northern Greenland, each of the twenty-two passengers was asking himself what he would discover during the trip.

One hundred years had passed since an important group of Baffin Land Eskimos had undertaken such a voyage. About 1856, a band of Tununirmiut had started a journey to the North under the guidance of Qidlak, a shaman. It is said that the latter, after bloody quarrels, had thought better for him to disappear and, on the occasion of a shaman ritual meeting, had taken advantage of his magic gift of flying to explore a far away country and to discover the Polar Eskimos—about whom he had heard shortly before from the explorer Inglefield. He described the promised land with such enthusiasm that many families decided to follow him.

About forty Eskimos left, but after a few years spent on Devon Island, some of them began to entertain doubts and the group divided itself. Only fifteen continued their north-ward journey and ended up, in 1860, by crossing Smith Sound and reaching Inglefield Land, where they mixed with the local population. Since then, there were only rare contacts between both sides of Baffin Bay, except for the 5th Thule Expedition (1921-1924), when Knud Rasmussen brought along to Canada a few Polar Eskimo families. Other isolated meetings had taken place at R.C.M.P. detachments on Ellesmere Island, where Eskimos, both from Pond Inlet and Thule were hired.

The remembrance of Qidlaq and his companions had not been lost on the Canadian coast. There was talk of another group which left Admiralty Inlet for Greenland about 1895, but information on what happened to them was contradictory.

For a number of years I had noted numerous testimonies on these migrations and I had read the narrative of Miqusaq, one of the migrants, in Rasmussen. However many areas remained in the dark and the best to clear them up was to go and learn on the spot what the Polar Eskimos knew about their ancestors.

On the other hand numerous Tununirmiut were anxious to renew their contacts with their cousins in Greenland. To organize a trip with these two objectives in mind was a splendid project for the Northwest Territories Centennial in 1970. My request for subsidies was accepted, but the project fell through as it was asked that the trip be made by dog-sled or ski-doo. To cross the rarely frozen Lancaster Sound by ski-doo was at least a hazardous venture. Going and coming back by dog-sled could not have been done during the same season.

The following year I contacted the N.W.T. Historical Advisory Committee and the Exchange Travel division of the Secretariate of State and both promised subventions. The project aborted again at the last minute when we were notified that the Danish Embassy required passports for all the travellers.

Finally, a year later, everybody took off, all in possession of valid passports. Two of our companions, descendants of Qidlaq's sister, had come by dog-sled from Iglulik, another from Arctic Bay. Many of the others were related to the migrants, or had previously met Polar

Eskimos. The trip that took Qidlaq and his group three years to make, we were to do it in two and one-half hours.

Contrary to what is generally observed on satellite photos, even taken in winter, we did not see any water between Pond Inlet and the Greenland coast. The winter having been extremely cold, it seems that the trip could have been made straight across and by dog-sled. It was only when nearing Thule that we noticed a few water holes.

At 11:00 hrs. (13:00 local time) we arrived in view of the Thule-Qânak village where a runway had been prepared for us on the ice. We had hardly landed when the majority of the people came to greet us. The hospitality shown to us from the beginning was to be one of the best memories of the whole trip.

Every one was immediately taken care of and those who were to spend all week there were taken to their hosts. At 15:00 hrs. everyone met in the community hall for a "kafemik" which, contrary to what the word implied, was an abundant banquet graced by pastries baked by the local ladies. The communal council president, August Eipe, whose words were translated in Danish and English, welcomed us. His homologue from Pond Inlet, Paniluk Sanguyak, expressed our joy at having finally made the trip and being acquainted with our Greenland "cousins" and gave thanks for the friendly reception. We noted with satisfaction that the Thule Eskimo dialect, different from that of Baffin Land, was close enough to it to entertain conversations.

There was someone who knew the Canadian Eskimos, and he was, in a way, the hero of the day, Porsiman, the "Bo'sun," alias Nasaitorluarssuk, had accompanied in 1921 the fifth Thule expedition to Canada and had been with Knud Rasmussen on the occasion of his memorable first meeting with Canadian Eskimos near Repulse Bay.

Nasaitordluarsuk—Porsiman—(Greenland)

Later, he accompanied Peter Freuchen to Pond Inlet and Arctic Bay, where the expedition's ship picked him up in 1924. A few of our companions had met him then. His fellow countrymen told us later that our visit had made him ten years younger.

At 17.00 hrs., half of our company was on its way back to Pond Inlet, accompanied by Polar Eskimo men and women, aged 22 to 77. Among them was Kale Peary, the explorer's son, and Kutsikitsoq, son of the noted Odak who accompanied Peary to the North Pole.

During the week we spent at Qânaq, we visited all the local institutions and installations and were given the desired information. There, as elsewhere in Greenland, the most important organization is the K.G.H. (State Commercial Society), whose director, Orla Sanborg, is at the same time Police Chief. Until 1963, Orla, who lived at Qânaq longer than any other white and who speaks the local dialect, was also president of the communal council. His responsibilities have now been divided: the Government has named an administrator—presently Nils Odgaard—and the council elects its own president. In four to six years, this council will have full administrative powers.

Six or seven Southern Greenlanders and about ten local Eskimos are at the service of the K.G.H. The store is quite busy and, what is more appreciated, prices are moderate. We noted, for instance, that gasoline is three times cheaper than at Pond Inlet. This is easy to explain when we are told that the K.H.G. is not authorized to make a profit, and even loses money every year. But this is not the only advantage for the Natives. Twice yearly, the fur pelts are sent to Copenhagen where they are sold at auction, and each hunter gets the surplus due him. The best hunters of the country thus have a substantial income.

Maigsanguaq and his wife Avortungiaq whose
grandfather came to Canada more than 100 years ago

We could not help compare Thule-Qânaq and Pond Inlet. All the Eskimos here—they number about 350—have frame houses. These are not as expensive as the ones the Canadian Government builds at Pond Inlet, but their occupants own them, buy their fuel and pay for their electricity. The Danish Government contributes 40% of construction costs and the Eskimos pay the balance at 5% a year. Electricity costs about 5 cents per Kw (12 cents at Pond Inlet) and fuel oil is about 20 cents a gallon (50 cents at Pond Inlet). On Canadian land, all—heat, electricity, water, services—are included in the rental, which is certainly not the best way to educate the people in saving money (the missions and a few other houses are about the only places where the lights are put out when not needed and where the doors are kept closed to economize on fuel). Taking into account the low prices at the store and the abundance of wildlife, there would be sufficient reason for a new migration to the East.

The Thule Eskimo enjoy family allowances. They receive old age pensions at 55 (it is likely that this will be raised to 65, as in the rest of Greenland). It appears that this favour was obtained by Knud Rasmussen, likely because of early mortality due to hard living conditions although our people were astounded at the great number of aged people at Qânaq.

Saturday evening we were served, in the community hall, a meal of raw maktaq (white whale or narwhal skin) which is considered a delicacy here as well as at Pond Inlet. I was expecting, not without apprehension, another delicacy special to the Polar Eskimo, "kiviak." In the spring when a species of small sea-birds come to nest by the thousands on the cliffs, they are caught with spoon-nets, stuffed with lard in sealskin jugs set on the rocks all summer long: the result is "kiviak" which tastes, I am told, like Roquefort cheese. I did not have a chance to taste it. At the end of meal, our hosts entertained us with songs in excellent mixed-voices. Then a film in Eskimo, on the Netjilit Canadian Eskimos, which I had brought along, was shown.

The next evening we offered, in our turn, a banquet of "quaq", frozen caribou meat and Arctic char from Pond Inlet.

At Qânak, water supply is entirely different from that of most Canadian Arctic settlements where water is hauled, summer and winter, by tankers, from a nearby lake and delivered to each home. Here, trucks haul iceberg ice. The supply is inexhaustible. I never saw so many icebergs in such a limited area. This ice is melted in a building near the shore from which hot and cold water is piped to the larger houses. A real technical success, since the village is built on a hillside, with the hospital at the summit.

Qânaq has a hospital, not simply a nursing station like Pond Inlet. Dr. Jappe Bohm is in charge, helped by his wife Marin, a nurse, and by several mid-wives and practical nurses. The hospital is large, with modern equipment. During my stay, a dentist came to spend some time. Unfortunately, teeth are in no better condition than on the coast of Baffin Land: twenty tons of sugar and 156,000 bottles of soft drinks are consumed yearly at Qânaq.

Qânaq is linked by radio to the neighbouring villages, and, when illness strikes, the doctor is advised without delay and can prescribe a cure. He has his own dog team and is able to go right away wherever he is needed. Notwithstanding my esteem for our Canadian doctors, I wonder if many of them would volunteer for this kind of work.

Inspection of a kamotik (Thule 1972)

I was anxious to know about education at Qânaq. The school principal, Christian Frederiksen, warmly welcomed us and showed us his large school. "When I was sent here," he said, "I was asked, according to the new school policy, to teach in Danish during the first years. I soon realized that this would not work. I learned Eskimo and explained everything in that language." Children attend school from seven to fourteen. The more gifted can pursue their studies in southern Greenland and, eventually, in Denmark. I entered several classrooms. In grade 5, Greenlandic was taught, that is, a southern dialect, the official language, that differs as much from the Thule dialect as the latter from the Canadian Eskimo. The children enjoy long holidays which allow them to accompany their parents on hunting expeditions. I did not see at Qânaq the bearded adolescent, hip-swaying and shifty-eyed, who is more and more common in the Canadian North. Here the youngsters are smiling and look at you straight in the eye.

Mr. Frederiksen, married to a southern Greenlander, has adopted, like many other Danes, certain local habits. He invited us to a delicious dinner of raw maktaq and frozen cariboo. The night before, we had been no less cordially received by the catechist-teacher Peter Jensen. The latter had built a small store where he sells local handicrafts, not taking any profit. Thus the prices are more reasonable than in Canada.

Orla Sandborg, who offerred me gracious hospitality, knowing the main purpose of my trip, had invited the best informants for an interview. Thus, I was able to question, among others, Inûterssuaq, specialist in local history, brother-in-law of Peter Freuchen and grandson of the immigrant Miqusaq whose adventures were related by Rasmussen. Inûterssuaq was able to throw some light on some obscure points in the history of the migration.

On the eve of our departure a dog-sled excursion was organized for those who wished to join. They were taken to the small village of Qeqertarssuaq (Herbert Island), situated across from Qânaq. Our travellers returned praising the local dogs but were less eulogious concerning the sleds. These are generally shorter and wider than those at Pond Inlet, and have two posts at the back. The transversal slats are very close and form a real floor on which the travelling Eskimo sleeps comfortably. There are still other differences: the whip is made of a wood handle about two feet long and, compared to the Tunnunirmiut, the strap is thinner. The dog traces are individual like ours, but are all of the same length. It is the authentic fan harnessing.

On April 14, the DC-3 was back, bringing back the Polar Eskimos who had left the previous week. About ten children from Pond Inlet were also on board, escorted by a teacher and a nurse. The children were received at the school and served lunch.

At the time of departure, a fair amount of the population gathered anew on the ice. The Danish and the Canadian flags were flapping side by side when John Scullion, administrator of Pond Inlet, expressed, on behalf of the Canadians, everyone's gratitude for the unforgettable reception given to them. The warmth of the farewell showed clearly that solid links of friendship had been forged between Greenlandic and Canadian Inuit.

A few more comments

Our Tununirmiut have lived in Greenland an experience they will never forget. For the first time, they have met people living in a natural milieu similar to theirs, but whose evolution is somewhat different. We have found at Thule-Qânaq men living in a country rich in wildlife and who seem determined—at least for the present—to exploit fully the natural resources of the land. They show a spirit of responsibility which struck us, adopting only among the modern technical innovations the ones which are fruitful. A striking example is the ski-doo which has replaced the dog team almost everywhere in the Canadian Arctic. Here, the ski-doo has been tried out, evaluated and rejected, its disadvantages outweighing its benefits. We only saw two at Qânaq. Their use is strictly regulated and it is forseeable that the local council will forbid entirely to drive them inside the limits of the village. After hearing the Inuit of Pond Inlet revving up their engines right in the settlement, Qânaq proved to be an oasis of calm and silence.

The Polar Eskimos, however, are not opposed to mechanization. In fact, they have more decked motorboats than their Canadian cousins. We counted a great number of them at Qânaq, three at Siorapaluk and four at Moriussaq. All have to follow strict regulations. There are areas rich in game where the use of motor boats is forbidden. Before the hunt, they anchor the boat, put their kayaks in the water and start chasing the narwhal, the beluga or the seal, harpooning at first the animal, then killing it with a lance or a gun. In Canada, however, one shoots first and harpoons the seal afterwards if it has not already sunk, which happens eight or nine times out of ten in summer. The Polar Eskimo shows a maturity concerning the preservation of the wildlife one would vainly look for in the Canadian North.

Many of those who in the past have been familiar with the Polar Eskimo notice the actual demoralization brought forth by urbanization and contacts with "civilization", even if many traditions still survive. Alcoholism is one of their most tragic problems. The solution brought by the Danes —at least in the Thule region—though not the best, has however limited the ill-effects of excessive drinking.

Everybody, White or Eskimo, has each month a number of points equivalent to so many bottles of beer or one bottle of whisky. Practically, on the first of the month, each one goes to the store to pick up his ration of booze and returns home to sacrifice it to Bacchus. The morning after, one has a hangover. During the remainder of the month the people show an exemplary sobriety! Total abstinence would probably be preferable, but when one sees Canadian Eskimos get whisky by the case, one cannot help think the Greenlandic solution is a step forward.

Concerning the school at Qânaq, it appeared better integrated to the village than those in the Canadian Arctic. They do not seek to introduce the child, at least in the beginning, to a world which is totally foreign. He is not enrolled, at age four, in a kindergarden as at Pond Inlet. Until he is seven, the family is the sole educator. He will not get his baccalaureate at sixteen, but he will likely be better equipped to live in his own country and he will avoid traumatic experiences. In one word, North-Greenland's policy is much wiser than the Canadian one, notwithstanding recent ameliorations to our system.

My Pond Inlet companions had already returned home. I had remained behind in Greenland in order to get more information. I visited Porsiman in the old folks home, I interviewed him at length. He answered my questions without hesitation, happy to recall Canadian memories. I showed him, in a photocopy of Peary's book, the picture of a woman carrying a child on her back. He had barely heard the woman's name that he exclaimed: "But, she is my mother. And I am the baby!"

On the 17th, I went to Siorapaluk with Kigutikkaq, thirty miles to the north. The dogs got us there quickly. The road was well travelled and there was very little snow as the annual precipitation here seems lower than at Pond Inlet.

Siorapaluk is a small village on a mountain side, with ten houses and 70 people. It has a small school and a store where essential goods are sold. The catechist was my gracious host. I visited the oldest man of the village, Immiinaq, whose grandmother had come from Canada with Qidlaq. He was about to harness his dogs to take his wife shopping at Qânaq, but knowing why I had come, he decided to postpone his trip so I could interview him. Many of the younger Inuit were away hunting bears. Contrary to what one would have thought, bears are not hunted to sell the skin but to use the skin to make trousers. Bearskin trousers are traditionally worn by Polar Eskimos. The women are not cheaply dressed either; they use blue and white fox skins for the upper garment and pants, and their high boots are bordered with bearskin.

Another very competent informant was Sakiungguaq who, before the war, had spent many years at the Police detachment on Ellesmere and Devon. He was able to inform me on the itinerary of ancient migrants. On the 19th we started on our way back. While Kiguttikkaq was harnessing his dogs, Sakiungguaq noticed that my mitts were not fit for the trip. He took them and put his own caribou-skin lining inside before putting them back on my hands. This is only but one example of the graciousness I experienced throughout my trip.

A U.S. enclave: the base of Thule

A U.S. Army helicopter brings the mail regularly to Qânaq. On the 21st of April, it took me to the base at Thule, with a brief stopover at Qeqertarssuaq, where Wally Herbert, the leader of the expedition which, a few years ago, travelled by dogsled from Alaska to Spitzbergen via the North Pole, had just spent the winter. The explorer was in

Canada, and I had met his wife and small daughter at Orla Sandborg's.

The flat-topped mountain which is the characteristic landmark in the country is well known by Eskimologists, since it adorns the cover of Knud Rasmussen expedition reports. It was just beside it that he had opened a trading post which was to be the point of departure of the "Thule expeditions." When the Americans came in 1951, it was still the most important centre for the Polar Eskimos. A few months later it was decided that the latter would settle at Qânaq which became for the Danes the new Thule, while the former village of Thule, located near the base was named officially Dundas.

This base, so much spoken of, and which at one time contained the whole deterrent nuclear power of the U.S.A., seemed to have lost much of its importance. Americans were now a minority, and mostly civilians. Half of the 2,000 population were Danish. In Thule, I met Father Haffely, a Catholic chaplain, who graciously looked after me during my stay and made me visit the local points of interest: two enormous radar screens directed to the North, the radio antenna, said to be as high as the New York's Empire State building, and the rocket sites, now dismantled. The base had also a very beautiful chapel serving the two major denominations.

In the base many buildings are now empty, some have been transformed into low cost hotels. Besides the military planes, a U.S. airline serves Thule and there is a weekly SAS flight from Copenhagen. Contrary to what I have seen too often in Canada, one does not meet, at Thule, Eskimos who wander aimlessly around. The Natives have kept their natural dignity. What I have seen, however, are blue foxes roaming the street fearlessly and hiding under the houses.

Father Haffely took me to visit "Dundas Village" where the Danish radio station is located. In the evening of the 24th, I showed there a film on the Netjilit Eskimos. Among the spectators was Qavigarssuaq, who previously like Porsiman, participated in the 5th Thule Expedition and accompanied Knud Rasmussen from Danish Island to Alaska, probably the longest trip by dog team ever attempted by Eskimos. Qavigarssuaq had just arrived from his village of Moriussaq, where I had decided to interview him. As he was to return the next day, I did not change my plans. On the 25th, the helicopter leaving for Qânaq took me to Moriussaq, a 20 or 25 miles away from the military base. Moriussaq is a small village of sixty people. Each family has built a platform on which there are one or two kayaks and a place to store the meat out of dogs' reach.

Qidlaq, the local teacher offered me hospitality. He is a grandson of Matt Henson, the American negro who accompanied Peary to the Pole. In 1968, I had met Qidlaq's brother at Godthab where he was studying. I also spent a delightful time with the local catechist, Ittukusuk, son of Qavigarssuak. He had in his home a picture of the Virgin; it shows the special devotion of the Lutheran Eskimos for Mary.

The next morning, I interviewed Qavigarssuaq (also known as Miteq). He had accompanied Rasmussen to Hikuligjuaq Lake, south of Baker Lake and had been at Chesterfield. The house we were in was in fact a house given to him by Knud Rasmussen himself. Later, he took me back by dog team to Dundas. In the evening, a violent blizzard activated "Phase 3" which means that, because of zero visibility, no one is allowed to go outside.

On the 28th, the storm calmed down, and the next morning, I bid my Greenlandic friends goodbye and I boarded a "Hercules" from the Canadian Air Force.

We had breakfast at the Alert meteorological station, the most northern inhabited point in the world , about 500 miles from the Pole. In the evening I was in Trenton, Ontario, back into agitation, noise, anonymous crowds—and darkness—early in April. At Thule the sun was shining all day.

For all, Inuit and Whites, the trip had been a memorable and enriching experience, because of what we had learnt and because of the atmosphere of friendship encountered from the first to the last day. At Pond Inlet, many have already asked me: "When do we go again to the country of the Akukiktut?[2]"

---

[2] In his acknowledgements, Father Rousselière thanked many people who had assisted him with his research, including his Igloolik and Northern Baffin informants, Anna Atagutsiaq, Inuujaq Qumangaapik, Sula Atagutsiaq Kublu, Letia Panipakutsuk, Aluluk, Ningiuq Qilirti, Simon Akpaliapik and Qanguq.

13

PARIS — ROME

On May 15, 1972, Father Mary-Rousselière flew to Europe. Realizing a dream that he had entertained for years and that now he could realize due to reduced plane fares, he took with him three of his parishioners, Alain Maktar and two of his children, Natalino, 18, and Katarina 16 years old. Were they bewildered at the change of scenery? Maybe, but they did not show any emotion when they boarded a Boeing 747 of Air France at the Montreal International Airport or, with Eurail passes in hand, criss-crossed the old European countries. Eyes wide open they were looking at everything and were slightly disappointed when at night they had to retire in their cabins, as it happened unfortunately between Toulouse, Carcassone and Marseille on the way to Rome. In the Eternal City, a fellow Oblate welcomed them and drove them, Italian style, to the General House of the Oblates of Mary Immaculate. They visited the most famous monuments of Rome, keeping unwritten notes in their prodigious memories. Monseigneur Sergio Pignedoli, Secretary of the Congregation for the Evangelization of the Nations, whom Father Rousselière had met at Pelly Bay in April 1965 while he was Pronuncio to Canada, opened the Propaganda Palace for them, with great gentleness and generosity in spite of a very full agenda. Monseigneur Pignedoli was not going to miss the film on the Inuit brought

Rome: (L. to R.) Natalino, Lucy Katarina, Antonio Ostan, o.m.i.
and Alain Maktar

by Father Rousselière. He would rather go without supper. Like his visitors, he contented himself with some sandwiches eaten during the presentation. On May 23, Monseigneur Clarizio, also a former Pronuncio to Canada and actually head of the Pastoral section concerning the Migrants, obtained for Father Mary and the Inuit a papal audience. The hall where Paul VI made his appearance, carried on the *sedia gestatoria,* was so large that it could have accommodate the whole Eskimo population of Canada. The official part of the audience finished, the Pope came to speak to them. Alain then gave the Pontiff a cross made of narwhal ivory and caribou antler. One of the most beautiful photographs taken on this occasion shows Paul VI, resting his two hands on Alain's shoulders.

Returning Via Aurelia to the Oblate House, the arctic travellers, after greeting Father Richard Hanley who had just succeeded Father Leo Deschâtelets as Superior General, participated at the closing banquet of the General Chapter which André Goussaert and myself had the honour to attend. At night, leaving Rome and its beautiful fountains, they took the train for Germany. "The crossing of Switzerland", wrote Father Mary, "reminded us of Baffin Land...with cows added!"

Arriving at Mayence, Germany, on May 25, they were greeted warmly by the Oblates. Among them, Father Schmitz Dominicus, a former classmate of Guy at La Brosse-Montceaux. The rain stopped them from taking a boat tour on the Rhine but not from going to Bingen where the Oblates were in charge of a very picturesque place of pilgrimage.

On the night of the 27th, they were again the guests of the Oblates, but this time in the capital of Denmark. The following day, a Sunday, Leif Zeillich-Jensen, the history

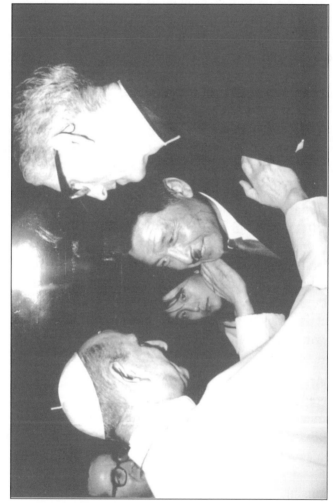

Papal audience with Paul VI: Alain Maktar and Guy Mary-Rousselière

professor at the University of Stockholm who had met Father Rousselière at Pond Inlet, unable to greet Father Rousselière in person, sent one of his friends, a very kind and distinguished lady, also a convert, to take them for a dinner in a chic restaurant of Copenhagen.They enjoyed it immensely.

Later they visited Jørgen Meldgaard, the well known Eskimologist, in his residence, a well managed farm with a thatched roof, about forty kilometres outside the city, in a region which is a real archaeological paradise with numerous tumuli of the Bronze Age. But what interested Natalino and Katarina most was to visit the stables and to see the first frolics of a little foal born the night before. This bucolic scene captivated them probably more than the collections of Eskimo art brought by Rasmussen, exhibited in the National Museum of Copenhagen.

Back in Paris, greeted at the North Railway Station by Monsieur Henri de Foucaucourt, a retired colonel, friend of the Oblates, who had spent a year at Igloolik, they began a western tour of France, visiting Chartres, Blois and Chambord before retiring for the night near Tours in the home of their gracious guide. The next morning, Alain and his son found the water of the swimming pool somewhat warmer than that of the lakes at Pond Inlet. In the afternoon, they enjoyed a visit to "Mont St. Michel" and stopped there for the night. On June 1, they headed for Falaise, a city in the Calvados region, famous for its violent combats in 1944, and then went to Lisieux to pray the Little Flower in her magnificent Basilica. Lisieux is not far fom Riviers, the birthplace of Monseigneur Turquetil. Arriving at Le Mans, they were shown a farm where the three Inuit saw for the first time the milking of the cows. Another time, they went to Solesmes to attend a High Mass celebrated at the Benedictine Abbey, renowned for its Gregorian chant.

Father Rousselière noticed the presence in the choir of many young monks. From there, they went to La Flèche, Sarthe, where the pastor of St. Colombe, a cousin of Father Mary, offered them lunch. After walking around the nearby zoo, leaving Mr. Henri, they returned to Pontoise by train. Pontoise is close to Paris and its attractions, Monmartre, Notre-Dame, the Eiffel Tower, just to mention a few. They had reserved the Sunday for a quiet family gathering. A few friends also came to share the little party. Among them was Father Jean-Marie Trébaol, a former missionary among the Inuit who had known Alain in the North when he was still a little boy. Because of his old age, Father Trébaol had retired in 1971 at Maffliers in the Parisian suburb, serving as chaplain for the Sisters of the "Manoir Notre-Dame". On Monday, after visiting the Louvres and the Château de Versailles, they answered to an invitation to dinner, preceded by a reception *au champagne* offered by Father Danielo's family at Maison-Alfort on the Marne. A wonderful evening! Meeting Alain and his children of whom "Uncle Etienne" had spoken so often was for his relatives an unexpected joy.

Tuesday June 6, 1972, Alain, Natalino and Katarina left from Orly to return to Canada while Father Rousselière flew to the East. Monsieur Henri had organized for him an exploratory trip under the patronage of Daniel Schlumberger, the Director of the French Archaeological Institute of Beyrouth, who received the Father very graciously at his home. The Sisters of Besançon had a convent near the Schlumbergers where Father Mary celebrated Mass every morning. Mr. Schlumberger was partially paralyzed, so his wife accompanied Father Rousselière to Damascus to visit the Souks and the Mosque of the Omeyyades, a seventh century Arab dynasty. Then, having crossed the desert by a road that was so broken up that it was better to drive beside it, they arrived in the unforgettable city of Palmyre, the City of Palms, with its stately ruins, the Temple of Bêl, its rich Necropolis and the valley of the tomb-towers between which at twilight an interminable herd of black goats passed through.When they returned Mrs. Schlumberger and Father Mary visited Hama with its creaking bucket-conveyors on the Oronte, the Krak of the Knights of the Crusades so well preserved that one could almost expect to see a troop of Knights come out with banners in the wind and lances on the ready. On June 10, they arrived at Beyrouth via Tripoli. The next day was spent visiting Byblos, the oldest city in the world, with its ancient and medieval fossils. After Byblos, Father Mary departed alone for Jerusalem where he was the guest of the Dominican Fathers of the Biblical School, among them were leading exegetes such as Fathers Benoit, Avril and Lelong. After a relatively quiet night, he walked the Via Dolorosa from the Ecce Homo Chapel to the Holy Sepulchre. He would have liked to have a few quiet moments to himself but the construction work at the basilica and the undisguised begging of certain representatives of the clergy were not conducive to prayer. In the afternoon he visited Bethlehem. He got lost in the labyrinthine paths of the old Jerusalem and could not find the wall of the lamentations. On the 15th, after climbing the Mount of Olives, he took the plane, stayed at Nicosie then arrived in Beyrouth at the home of his good friends, the Schlumbergers. From there, he went for a short trip to Saïda or Sidon, and then had to leave his guests, deeply touched by their warm welcome. It was with great sorrow that in November 1972, he learned of the sudden death of Mr. Schlumberger. The Professor was lecturing at Princeton University, U.S.A., when he passed away.

Pond Inlet—Arctic Research

Beautiful days are always too short. On June 29, Father Mary flew from Orly to Montreal and on July 10, he arrived at Pond Inlet, via Resolute Bay, accompanying the German Ambassador to Canada who had come to visit Hermann Steltner. Hermann was a Canadian of German descent in charge of the logistic for an expedition of German scientists of the University of Münster working together with students from Brock University of St. Catherines in Ontario. He had founded the *Establishment of the Arctic Research* with as its speciality, the study of the sea ice. This was a very important matter considering that some Ruhr industrialists wanted to buy the iron extracted at Mary River and transport it in giant freighters built to brave the ice fields.

On the 26th of July, the sea was still solidly frozen and Father Mary left by dog team with Qaunaq heading for Button Point. Another Inuk, Nutarak, followed them by skidoo, transporting the camping equipment. Georgia was also a part of the expedition; she was the daughter of an American General who was present with Clark at the notorious rendez-vous of Algiers. She is known as "Georgia", without any family name and she considers the North as her adopted country. For many years, she worked as cook for the Churchill mission, then resided at Repulse Bay in a small government house normally rented to the Inuit before moving to Igloolik. In 1982, she published her memoirs entitled *Georgia, An Arctic Diary*. And now, together with Father Rousselière, she dreamed of archaeological discoveries but the weather was not very favourable. It was cold and the snow was still falling at the end of July. The result of their excavation consisted of a few wooden statuettes very seldom found elsewhere.

Arctic Archaeologists attending the Santa Fe Conference, 1972

Back row—Dr. Albert A. Dekin, Jr., Dr. William Kemp, Dr. William Fitzhugh, Fr. Guy Mary-Rousselière, o.m.i., Dr. Robert McGhee, Dr. Ronald J. Nash. Front row—Dr. James A. Tuck, Dr. Moreau S. Maxwell, Dr. Elmer Harp, Jr., Dr. William E. Taylor, Jr.

229

Twice the plane attempted a landing to pick them up, but twice, it failed. The runway was too soft and the plane was not equipped with the appropriate balloon tyres. Finally they had to return to Pond Inlet by canoe, following the shore or navigating between the ice floes, arriving on August 26. The year 1972 was an exceptional year for ice, so exceptional that the Inuit had never seen anything like it since 1922. Nevertheless, the ice did not stop the boats from bringing supplies for the community. In fall, the sea froze early and a thick layer of snow rapidly covered the new ice so nobody could guess its thickness with the result that in November several skidoos went through it, fortunately without loss of life. In the same period, in the semi-darkness, a teacher returning from a caribou hunt, shot and narrowly missed his companion Inukuluk, having mistaken him for a polar bear.

Ataata Mari was away excavating when to his great sorrow, his good friends the Scullions moved to Cape Dorset. Their departure left a great emptiness in the settlement. However, winter came and went very rapidly. Father Mary had at the request of the School of American Research to prepare a paper on Arctic archaeology to be delivered at Santa Fe, New Mexico. He had to develop the characteristics of the Pre-Dorset and Dorset civilizations. All expenses paid, he arrived in Santa Fe, February 1973, and presented his research to a small group of Canadian and American scientists, gathered under the chairmanship of Professor Moreau S. Maxwell of the University of Michigan. They were all sitting around the fireplace in the living room of a real Mexican Adobe home. Santa Fe had all the characteristics of a beautiful little Spanish city built at more than 2000 m. of altitude and was still surrounded by snow. Father Rousselière visited there the oldest church in the United States. He went also about a hundred kilometres further north to visit in the mountains the *"Pueblo de Taos"*, the region where Pueblo Indians still live in their traditional superimposed houses.

Father Rousselière brought back only happy memories of his trip, but soon after his arrival at Pond Inlet early March he caught the English flu virus. His fever rose a full degree when he learned that his Oblate Provincial Superior suggested that he take charge of the mission at Chimo, Nouveau Quebec. Barely recovered, he preferred to fly to Arctic Bay where the Paniaks, a Catholic family from Igloolik, had come to spend the winter.

Chesterfield Inlet

In May 1973, the Hudson Bay missionaries were invited to Chesterfield to celebrate the Golden Jubilee of Father Ducharme, nick-named Mikilar, who had come from Arviat. Fifty years earlier, on August 3, 1923, he was ordained priest by Bishop Ovide Charlebois of The Pas. A retreat and a seminar animated by Martin Roberge, Oblate of St. Paul University, Ottawa, followed Mikilar's day. Long discussions tended to develop the meaning of missionary life, the building of a local Church respectful of Inuk identity and of socio-economic and cultural changes now invading the North. The scientific work of Father Mary-Rousselière, his scholarly relationships with his colleagues in anthropology, his friendly contacts with Inuit, often non-catholics, were considered of primary importance. Even the Inuktitut translation of the *Eskimo* magazine was suggested, as well as the use of his slide collection to illustrate the diocesan catechesis and to help the formation of the religious leaders trained in Pelly Bay.

During the same month of May 1973, Father Rousselière came to Ottawa where an exhibition of prehistoric and modern Inuit art was held at the National Gallery.

The National Museum of Man in Ottawa asked him to film and supervise, once back in Pond Inlet, the construction of a kayak[1]. To this end, he borrowed some sophisticated photographic equipment from the National Film Board. Two renowned kayakers, Nutarak and Kumangapik, built the wooden structure; some Inuit women chewed and cut the skins to cover it. The work was done in the school that was closed for summer holidays. The school located at the other extremity of the village forced Ataata Mari to walk back and forth many times a day, not wanting to miss filming any significant steps in the procedure.

In June, he spent ten days at Button Point in the company of Qaunaq, a good man whose only fault was to snore like a regiment of fire fighters. Without much success at the archaeological level, they however enjoyed the trip looking at seals basking in the sun.

In July 1973, he welcomed Jean-Louis de Gerlache de Gomery[2], a charming man who would accompany him in his summer excavations. Jean-Louis'grandfather, Baron Adrien de Gerlache, born in Hasselt, Belgium, in 1866, directed the *Belgica* expedition to Antarctica (1897-1899) and was the first to winter there. Jean-Louis'father, Captain Gaston de Gerlache de Gomery, was the leader of the 1957 Belgian expedition to Antarctica. The cold

---

[1] Cf. *Contributions to Kayak Studies* edited by E.Y. Arima, page 41 to 72: *Report on the Construction of a kayak at Pond Inlet in 1973* by Father Guy Mary-Rousselière, illustrated with 16 photographs.

[2] Cf. *Les Gerlache. Trois générations d'Explorateurs Polaires*, (1897-1997), by Charles E.Schelfhout. Editions de la Dyle, Belgium. Chapter XX, *En Arctique (1973-1988)*.

Guy Mary-Rouselière holding two narwhal ivory tusks

Guy Mary-Rousselière in his tent at Nunguvik

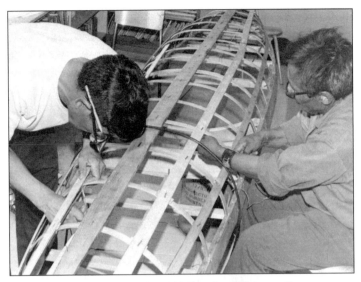

Construction of a kayak by Nutarak and Kumangapik
(Photo used to illustrate the article written by Guy Mary-Rousselière,
p. 55, in *Contributions to Kayak Studies* edited by E. Y. Arima)

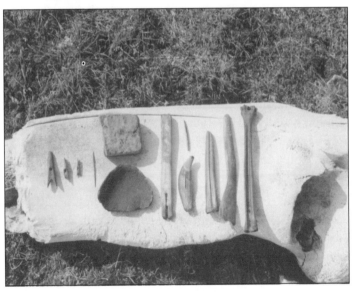

Nunguvik

countries are truly a tradition of the family. In spite of a spell of nephritis which hit Father Mary,—once every forty years, he said—, soon alleviated successfully by medication dropped from a plane, the discoveries proved to be interesting. A small portable transmitter allowed him to keep contact with Pond Inlet. The weather was usually fair until the day a violent storm arose that overturned Jean-Louis' tent and flooded Ataata Mari's.

Early September, Jean-Louis de Gerlache left the North via Resolute Bay and Little Cornwallis Island where a lead and zinc mine was in operation. Exploratory drillings for oil were also carried in the arctic archipelago by the Panarctic Company. The Inuit hired to help were employed for a period of twenty days followed by ten days at home, a stay long enough to attend to their traditional occupations, like hunting and fishing.

The modest Catholic community of Mittimatalik increased slightly with the addition of a family arriving from Igloolik. The chapel was manifestly becoming too small and Father Rousselière drew some plans for a new building. Bishop Robidoux was suggesting trailer type or mobile home, an idea which did not please him too much because a similar experience attempted in Arctic Bay had proven negative. However, after the catechists meeting at Pelly Bay in January 1974, held almost entirely in Inuktitut, he accepted to go down to Montreal to see and eventually to order such a trailer.

He was barely back at Pond Inlet when a call from Resolute Bay advised him of the death of Bob Brûlé, one of his parishioners and the manager of the Coop store. Bob had burned in the fire which destroyed his house. Was it due to too much Saturday night partying or to a cigarette not entirely put out, who knows? In any case, it was a very sad news for Father Mary who had in 1972 at Pond Inlet blessed the marriage of his friend Bob with an Inuk lady. Now Mrs Brûlé and her two year old son were left rather in poverty. As for the victim, the body was sent to Frobisher for an autopsy and to Montreal for the burial. May he rest in peace!

At the beginning of April 1974, around Easter, Dr. Cornelius Remie, a Dutch anthropologist came to spend a week with Father Rousselière. He was a disciple of Geert Van den Steenhoven, the law specialist of the Keewatin Eskimos. Dr.Remie was busy translating the diary of Bernard Iqugaqtuq under the guidance of Father Vandevelde, staying in the mission of Hall Beach with his family.

In May 1974, Richard, the one year old son of Joanna, a young Pond Inlet mother, died of meningitis. The body was sent to Iqaluit for an autopsy and then returned to the family at the beginning of June. Father Rousselière dressed in the white vestments customarily worn for funerals of young innocent children conducted in good faith the burial of the baby. It was later learned that a mistake had been made on the identity of the child... a case for Saint Peter to solve at the gates of heaven.

During the same month of May, he attended the missionary congress organized jointly by the Oblates of the Mackenzie and Hudson Bay dioceses held in Fort Smith concerning the pastoral approach needed to face modern times. The meeting was darkened with the news of Father Franche's assassination in Aklavik and also by the sickness of Father Métayer suffering from cancer. Already he had a leg amputated and his condition was deteriorating rapidly. Father Rousselière paid him a visit at the Camsell Hospital in Edmonton. They had been good friends for many years.

Returning to Pond Inlet on May 31st, he found the country hidden under a thick blanket of snow. Canada geese arriving approximately at the same time from the south, seemed lost and had to delay the construction of their nests. This discouraged Doug Heyland, the biologist who came every spring to study their habitat.

In June, those who were to help him in the excavations at *Nunguvik* and *Saatut* arrived from various points of the globe. From France, Dr. Michel Brahic, virologist, assistant at the Faculty of Marseille, with his wife Beverly who was of English Canadian descent and their ray of sunshine, their ten month old daughter Anne. From Belgium, an engineer, Arnould d'Oultremont, recruited by Jean-Louis de Gerlache, after having completed his studies in London, England. From Austria, Walter Hannak, a student in medicine and psychiatry. Finally from Canada, Susan Rowley, 17 year old daughter of Graham Rowley whose friendship with Father Mary has already been mentioned. A first attempt by plane to reach *Nunguvik* failed because of the soft condition of the runway. The second try aborted before it even started, the plane having crashed at Arctic Bay, luckily without human casualty. Finally on July 12, the flight was successful and the "digging crew" started to work, soon followed by hordes of voracious mosquitoes whose continual annoying buzzing diminished the pleasure of the search. Dr. Brahic, his wife and Anne left on the 19th, very proud of their finds: a small statuette, its head adorned with horns, a microblade and a burin with its handle made of wood and bone tied together with caribou sinew and very well preserved.

On August 10, at the *Arnakadlak* site, when everyone was slowly and carefully digging, Nutarak came running and shouting: "*Nanualuk!*" "A big bear!" They all stood up and saw the bear come to a dead stop at a distance of about 150 metres. He was turning his head left and right, probably appraising the situation; then, he ran a short

Guy Mary-Rousselière sitting on a narwhal. (One of the Inuit is Kayak)

Kayak's mother

distance towards the north and stopped. Attracted by the smell of old narwhals carcasses, the king of the tundra came back and standing on his hind legs on top of a little knoll, he observed, according to Father Mary's remark, "the strange bipedes that we are!" Nutarak scared him away by firing his gun without trying to hit him. The bear walked then to the beach where the expedition's supplies were stacked and feasted on pilot biscuits. Another time a bear came along and had fun pulling to pieces the rubber boat of the excavators. One day, Kayak was returning to his boat with a kettle full of soft water when suddenly he had a feeling that a polar bear was following him. He ran and just made it to the boat, heading as fast as he could for deep water. Regarding the killing of polar bears, the Inuit, in general, respected the law and knew that they were not to shoot more than the 13 bears allowed annually to the local hunters of Pond Inlet, a quota often reached early in the spring.

Bishop Robidoux had decided to equip all his missions with a safe where objects of value and official papers could be stored and sheltered against fire, theft or even the curiosity of some unscrupulous visitors. With a touch of humour, Father Guy had written his Bishop that if he wanted him to use the safe, he had better send him a house to put around it! When returning to Pond Inlet at the end of August, to his great surprise, he found that not one but two trailers had arrived during his absence, one to serve as chapel and the other as living quarters. Unable to manage by himself, Father called to help the crew which had arrived to work for the government. The men, free only at night after their regular hours, levelled the ground, built a bed of gravel and placed on it the two trailers. They also installed the heating system and the electricity. Everything should have been perfect, except that one trailer had been seriously damaged during the unloading and that both appeared to be

The two trailers sent to Pond Inlet to replace the old mission, (1974)

of very poor craftsmanship, if not just bungled by the ATCO factory where strikes were threatening at the time of the construction.

From September to November, Brother Jérôme Vermersch came from Gjoa Haven to fix everything that was defective, the water main, the bathroom plumbing, the insulation of the walls, just to enumerate a few. Father Rousselière was under the impression that he had moved from an old decrepit building to a real palace, with even an extra room for visitors. He had a personal phone installed and via the Anik satellite told his sister Béatrice of his intention to visit France sometime in April 1975, at least if, through daily physiotherapy, he could get rid of a very annoying hygroma, commonly called bursitis.

14

OVERSEAS TRAVEL

In the first days of January 1975, Father Rousselière was invited to Ottawa to meet some of the leading scientists at the National Museum to discuss the "Thule Project". This project consisted of a group of people interested in archaeology anxious to go north during the summer. If landing in Pond Inlet, would Father allow them to stay in the old mission presently empty? The answer was obviously affirmative.

In April, he left Pond Inlet for holidays in France, hopping from one stopover to the next. First in Igloolik where he arrived almost at the same time as Father Fournier, the hermit of *Ikpik,* returning from a preaching tour in the missions of the diocese. In *Sanerajak,* at Father Vandevelde's residence, he interviewed two elders, Ivalak and Amimiarjuk, both having known Rasmussen. At *Iqaluit*, he found the city all decorated and flags flapping in the wind to honour the Prince of Wales who had arrived the day before.

After greeting his family in France, he crossed over to England to visit his nieces. Touring the country, he was filled with wonder before the magnificent Anglican Cathedral of Worcester. He also witnessed the changing of the guard in front of Buckingham Palace. At Cambridge, Jean-Louis de Gerlache who was preparing a B.A. in

Economics had him visit the ancient and famous University. On this occasion, the Father admired the keen sense of tradition and decorum of the English. Hugh Brody, an Oxford graduate and author of many books on the Inuit, next piloted him to the "Scott Polar Research Institute" where Dr. Armstrong welcomed him warmly and showed him documents related to the 19th century expeditions. Someone even played, in his honour, a small mechanical organ that was in Sir William Edward Parry's cabin and on which he entertained the Eskimos of Igloolik in 1823.

Back in his native country, on May 15, he met some former classmates, many of them he had not seen for 45 years, and dined with them in the "Little Seminary" at Paris. At Marseille, with Michel and Beverly Brahic who had accompanied him last year in the *Nunguvik* excavations, he visited the ancient Abbey of Senanque built by the Cistercians in the 12th century. At Aix-en-Provence, he was welcomed in the very cradle of the Oblate Congregation.

Later in May, he met, in Holland, Cornelius Remie, professor at the University of Nijmegen and Geert Van den Steenhoven, both mentioned earlier. Naturally, the situation of the Church in Holland was one of their main topics of discussion. They regretted to see married priests allowed to teach Theology in a Catholic university, blaming the lack of authority on the part of the Dutch bishops. Father Rousselière had always been the defender of orthodoxy, never hiding his opinions. For instance, he would not introduce in his mission the innovative rite of distributing the Holy Communion in the hand, although he was open-minded enough not to refuse the Consecrated Bread to whomever presented his hand instead of his tongue. He justified his attitude saying that often the hands of the recipients were not exactly clean and that the fact of receiving in the hand could often denote a lack of respect and faith in the Real Presence. He was horrified to learn that some priests did not believe anymore in the Presence of Christ in the Eucharist, once the Mass was over. "It seems to me," he said, "that if someone could persuade me to believe that the Church for twenty centuries has literally stuffed our heads full of ideas on such an important point, she would lose all credibility and I would leave her immediately." Luckily, his faith was as strong as the rock on which the Church is built and he was full of admiration for the Lutheran Eskimos of Thule who received Holy Communion kneeling down. Maybe some will consider him as behind his time, slightly obsolete, when he was just trying to be faithful to the directives received from Rome. He did not really know what to think of the French clergy, although he had the clear impression that a great number of priests "had fallen on their head", that the children were not catechized and that the people in general no longer knew whom or what to believe! However he found hope and comfort at the sight of young couples who promised fidelity to God, to the Church and to each other.

Later during his holidays, he paid a visit to his former Provincial Superior, Father Haramburu of Casteljaloux. Together, by a very special favour, they visited the Grotto of Lascaux, discovered in 1940 but presently closed to the public in order to prevent the proliferation of micro-organisms attacking the wall paintings dating many centuries before Christ. They also visited Eyzies, en Dordogne, the Capital of the pre-history, but at noon, only restaurants were open, museums and grottos were closed.

On the way back to Pontoise, Guy stopped in Le Mans, his birthplace. Memories of his youth surfaced. From his cousins' apartment, he could see the "Garden of Plants" where he had often played as a child.

On June 4, he left for Belgium. He visited the Gerlache family in their castle of Mullem where he found so much arctic memorabilia that, for a while, he had the impression he was back in Northern Canada.

Taking advantage of his Eurail Pass, he reached Copenhagen, welcomed with open arms by Jørgen Meldgaard. In Sweden, he greeted Leif Zeillich-Jenzen who had just published a book on Eskimo beliefs and who was also very apprehensive of the marxist materialism invading his government.

Father Mary arrived in Innsbruck, Austria, in the middle of a popular feast. Alas, too late to see the parade of the Tyrolian hunters in their red costumes! Walter Hannak, another companion of the previous year at *Nunguvik*, guided him in a short tour of the city, then drove him to the convent of the Jesuit Fathers at the University of Innsbruck. It was the day of the annual banquet of the Jesuits and of course they invited their visitor to share their table. "I was the only one", he wrote later, " to wear the roman collar and I felt like a duck in the middle of chickens!"

Finally, the wings still intact, the duck landed at Pond Inlet on June 20. At the beginning of July, Jean-Louis de Gerlache came again to help Father Mary-Rousselière to excavate the Inuit past. On July 7, they departed by plane for *Nunguvik*. The pilot, an Inuk by the name of Markusi, unfortunately landed on bumpy ground outside the runway. The front wheel broke and the plane came to a grinding halt on its nose. No one was injured and work started as usual.

A few days later, Father Mary's cousin, Didier Bertrand, arrived escorted by archaeologists from the National Museum, Dr. McDonald, Director of the Archaeological Survey of Canada, and Dr. McCartney, Director of the Thule Project. Father Rousselière was delighted to accompany

Nose dive at Nunguvik

them on an air-reconnaissance flight and, in spite of the bumpy ride, to photograph different sites in the region.

At the beginning of August, another visitor, rather unwelcome, approached his tent. "What a queer sensation", he wrote, "to awaken and feel the paws of a polar bear on one's shoulders!" So he decided that in the future he would take a dog with him to keep *nanuk* away. Why not choose a goose? After all, geese had long ago protected Rome! J.L.Freund, a film producer who had come to film the geese on Bylot Island brought him five goslings, very alive, and asked him if, once back at Pond, he would take good care of the little orphans. Of course, he agreed and soon had the pleasure to show them to Pierre Elliot Trudeau, the Prime Minister of Canada, and to his son, Justin, who were passing through Pond Inlet with Stuart Hodgson, the Commissioner of the Northwest Territories. Both, the Prime Minister and the Commissioner, showed great interest in archaeology and expressed their sincere appreciation for the work done under the supervision of Father Mary. After reading an article written by Father Rousselière in the "National Geographic", Pierre Trudeau sent him these lines: "The excellent article you published, eloquently synthetizes your intimate knowledge of the Eskimo people whose life you have already shared for thirty years."

Pond Inlet continued to develop. Television had already arrived. The telephone via the satellite was functioning normally, allowing transcontinental communications. When Father Vandevelde came in October to pay a visit to Father Mary, his confrère and friend, he phoned Belgium and got the latest news from his relatives. Father Vandevelde had flown in with the plane bringing to Pond Inlet the members of Inuit Tapirisat of Canada who had their meeting at Mittimatalik to discuss territorial claims. The debates were in Inuktitut with more or less adequate simultaneous translation for the benefit of the legal advisers and other non-Inuit participants. The three Pelly Bay representatives, Barthelemy, Simon and Henry stayed at the old mission. Henry Uqarluk was to die the same year in November; he had been hunting and on the way home, his skidoo went through thin ice and he drowned.

More Meetings

At the end of February 1976, Father Mary-Rousselière went to Igloolik to participate at the meeting of missionaries, Inuit catechists and delegates of the parish councils coming from the north zone. Then, he went to Ottawa where he had the pleasure of meeting a young French ethnologist, Jean-François Le Mouël, disciple of Leroi-Gourhan and Director of the Arctic Department of the Museum of Man in Paris. Le Mouël was preparing an expedition to the Canadian North, including *Nunguvik*.

In May, he took part, at least for a short while, at the Oblate meeting bringing together the Hudson Bay and Keewatin missionaries in the beautiful retreat house of St. Mary's province at Saskatoon. The grass was green, the birds were singing, the river Saskatchewan was running its murky water alongside the property. The welcome from the personnel of the house was as warm as the sun in springtime.

The trip home to Pond Inlet took him through Edmonton and Resolute Bay with a stopover of a week in Arctic Bay. Around Easter, the trailer of the school principal, similar to the ones the Father was living in, was destroyed by fire during his absence. Everything went up in smoke, including books, documents on the Arctic and regretfully, the preparatory material for a book.

During summer, instead of excavating, he put all his notes in order having been asked by the National Museum to publish the results of his research. Just as well he did not go away. In July, Kayak, one of his best friends, died suddenly at the age of 57. Ataata Mari and Kayak were often seen together. When not digging for artifacts, they were discussing religion. Former Special Constable, he was probably the most decorated Inuk in Canada. Many R.C.M.P. and Government personalities attended his funeral. The bugle sounded the last post and six wreaths covered his coffin.

Father Rousselière was seldom alone. Unable to take a group of Americans, members of the Minnesota Historical Society, to an excavation site, the season being too advanced, he gave them a lecture and showed them slides. In September, he received the visit of his provincial, Father Robert Lechat[1] from Igloolik. Both great gentlemen and known scholars, but not necessarily always of the same opinion, no doubt the little trailer did witness some hot but always friendly discussions.

In October, Father Mary paid another visit to Arctic Bay. Having sold to the local Coop the small building that served as a mission, he no longer had there a "pied-à-terre". He gratefully accepted the hospitality offered by the school teacher, Mike Pembroke and his family, saying mass in their living room, large enough to accommodate all the 26 Catholic Inuit.

---

[1] Robert Lechat, French Oblate born in 1920. From 1946 to 1972, missionary in the Diocese of Labrador-Schefferville. From 1972 to 1994, missionary at Igloolik and Sannerajak in the Churchill—Hudson Bay Diocese. Now retired in the Deschâtelets Edifice in Ottawa, translating and editing liturgical text in Inuktitut and making trips North to assist in the missions at Christmas and Easter.

Presently, his pastoral care also included the personnel of the Strathcona mine, called *Nanisivik* in Inuktitut. The mine had just begun extracting zinc and lead, together with a small amount of silver. The ore was stored in a huge warehouse and during the navigation season directly loaded on freighters coming alongside the wharf and then departing for foreign countries like Germany. *Nanisivik* was at that time linked to Arctic Bay, 30 kilometres away, by a mountainous road quite dangerous in stormy weather, having no traffic signs, no guide-posts and no deflectors. Among the 28 families working at the mine, several were French Canadian and four were Inuit. That particular Sunday, the attendance at Mass was rather sparse as the night before there had been a Halloween Ball conducted by the "Iceberg Orchestra" of Arctic Bay. Since the opening of the mine's facilities, Anglican and Catholic priests agreed to have only one chapel for both denominations. Presently, they were enjoying free room and board in the hotel. The food was excellent. However, Father Mary broke one of his teeth, and to have it repaired, had to fly to Iqaluit. A journey that cost approximately four hundred dollars. Dr. Marc Levesque, the resident dentist, fixed the tooth and even invited Ataata Mary for a family dinner at his home. When he returned to Pond, Father found out that he had two more teeth broken! Did it happen when having dinner at the dentist's table or when eating frozen caribou meat at the mission in company of Father Joseph Choque? He was not sure! Father Choque knew Father Mary very well. He offered him a small black and white TV set. "I do not risk," wrote Father Rousselière, "to pass for a millionnaire, when most of the natives own coloured sets!" And reflecting on the past, he added: "When I stop and think what life was like thirty years ago, with mail only once a year and a few rare radio messages, this is really another world!" The old Atuat of Arctic Bay,

253

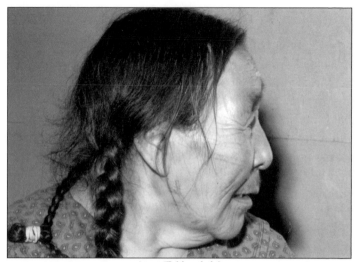

Atuat (Eskimo lady)

Kayak's mother and his family

the eldest and probably the last tattooed lady in Baffin Land, will not be there anymore to talk about the past with Father Mary for she had gone to join her ancestors, unless if, according to an old Eskimo belief, she would reincarnate in one of her grandchildren.

In April 1977, a sorrowful crime rocked the community of Pond Inlet. The late Kayak's daughter, about 30 years old, was stabbed in her sleep by her brother who was suffering from a mental disturbance. The man, a menace for the whole community, would have been, years ago, executed by his fellow Inuit to remove the fear gnawing at the camp.

Priest—Writer

On June 14, 1977, the colleagues of Father Rousselière at Saint Sulpice in Paris planned a reunion to underline the 40th anniversary of their ordination to the priesthood. Ataata Mari mentioned the event to his Bishop and to his religious superior, Father Lechat, and both agreed that he should go to France to partake in the celebration.

Before flying to Europe, he went to see his doctor in Sherbrooke and soon after, he underwent an operation of the prostate, "the very same operation Charles de Gaule had to go through", said he with humour. His hospitalization prevented him attending the Archaeological Congress in Ottawa where a substitute read the paper he had written for the occasion.

Having been given the green light from his doctor, he arrived in France on the 23[d] of May, right in the middle of a general strike. As usual, he visited his family and his friends in England, Belgium, Denmark and Holland without, of course, forgetting the 40th anniversary celebration in Paris, the main reason for his trip.

Later, when flying home to Pond Inlet, he met four biologists from the University of Strasbourg, veterans of Spitzberg and Alaska, anxious to study arctic wildlife on Bylot Island.

On July 9, 1977, by plane, he went to *Nunguvik* with Georgia who had arrived from Igloolik and Louise Pettigrew, a lady from Montreal. The weather was perfect and the discoveries interesting, making him conclude that at one undetermined date Baffin Land had somewhat tipped over! Inspired by Inuit psychology and the habits of the polar bear, Ataata Mari had with him two dogs in order to keep Nanuk at a safe distance until their return to Pond Inlet on the 21st of August.

Not long after their arrival in the settlement, Jean-Louis de Gerlache came to visit Father Rousselière, arriving by plane from Gjoa Haven via Resolute Bay. During the summer, Jean-Louis and Willy De Roos, a Dutchman living in Belgium, had sailed aboard the *Williwaw* from Egedesminde, Greenland, to King William Island through the North-West Passage. Being too late for the excavations at *Nunguvik*, Jean-Louis, anxious to live the life of a real Eskimo, went along with Nutarak to the *Kurluktuk* river to fish for Arctic Char. Twelve days later, they brought back for the benefit of the Pond Inlet people several bags of big and delicious fish.

In 1978, on the 6th of July, the day he turned 65, Father returned to *Nunguvik*. He was accompanied by two young Belgian ladies, Henrianne de Gerlache, sister of Jean-Louis, and her friend Sophie de Ligne. Accompanying them was an American gentleman, a former Marine Major, who two years before had sailed from Arctic Bay to Pond Inlet by kayak and his friend, Ed Jordan. Father had known Ed more than 30 years ago at

Arctic Bay where he was radio operator and later on the Dew Line where he had been appointed station chief. At the excavation site, the white geese were so numerous that one had to watch where one walked! Still, there was enough space left for the Petro-Canada helicopter to land safely, bringing the mail and flying the excavators over the magnificent glaciers of Bylot.

It is not enough to dig and to find artifacts. From time to time, you have to sit and evaluate your discoveries. That is exactly what Father Mary did when, with the help of a grant from the Social Sciences and Humanities Research Council, he spent two of the winter months at the National Museum in Ottawa, examining under a strong microscope the minute points of burins. He was easily recognizable among the scientists because of his roman collar which always showed that he was a priest first and foremost.

He had also brought with him from the North some samples of human hair which, he thought, were of the Dorset and Thule periods. He submitted them to the scrutiny of the R.C.M.P. laboratory, together with some specimens of animal hair which were identified as coming from muskox, defeating the theory of some scientists saying that the ovibos had never existed on Baffin Land. More sophisticated tests made at the laboratory of Rochester, U.S.A., according to the mercury content of the hair, could even determine the exact age of the muskox and even find out its diet.

Commenting on the news that a piece of painted wood dating from the year 1280 had been found at *Nunguvik*, Father pointed out that recent excavations on Ellesmere had uncovered fragments of coats of mail, pieces of material and other vestiges of Viking origin also from the 13th century. He could not help making this remark: "It is piquant", he wrote "to think that the cousins far removed of my Norman grandfather's ancestors could have, long ago, come to the Canadian Arctic!"

Father Rousselière returned North in December, finding the mission in a very sad state, with the water pipes and the reservoir solidly frozen. The place took a long time to warm up and without a doubt he had to rub his hands to keep them warm, walking back and forth in the hall of his mobile home, thinking of his job as editor of *Eskimo*. The magazine worried him very much. The translations were not always accurate and the grammatical and spelling errors too numerous to his liking. Most of the articles were left to his own initiative. He published short biographies of departed missionaries, for instance the life of Bishop Lacroix who died on September 9, 1976; the continuation of Father Buliard's diary; the story of Father Lucien Schneider, missionary, linguist and grammarian who died in Paris June 6, 1978. The deaths affecting the Hudson Bay Diocese were many in 1979. Father Mary asked me to write the obituaries of Father Henry, deceased on February 4, 1979 and of Father Ducharme who died on September 29 that same year. Knowing how difficult it is for a brother to talk about his brother, tactfully, he wrote the necrology of my brother, Father Joseph Choque, who died of lung cancer on March 4, 1979, in Richelieu, Québec. He also composed an article on Brother Romeo Boisclair who, on November 20, 1979, did not wake up from a nap he was having in his office in the basement of the Chesterfield hospital.

Father Mary-Rousselière continued to offer well thought editorials regarding the education and the problems of the youth in the North. He also widened the horizon of his readers offering them the epic of the Jesuit missionaries in Alaska. He published the courageous odyssey of the Grey Nuns on the 50th anniversary of the foundation of St. Therese's Hospital, (1931-1981), as described in the articles of Sister Yvette Paquin, the archivist for the Grey Nuns at Nicolet.

He did not mince words to denounce the civilization of waste that suddenly hit the Inuit, challenging their own culture, a culture well adapted to the surroundings and which had, more or less, remained unchanged for centuries. Evidently, he did not deny the past influence of the whalers, the traders and the missionaries. He did not try to excuse the slaughter of caribou and muskox, due to the introduction of the gun and often executed at the request of the white men. He came to the conclusion that the facility for the modern Inuk to buy clothing and food from the store merely multiplied the needs of the traditional hunter. The introduction of money among the Natives did not improve their perception of values, neither their desire to save for hard times ahead. When in urgent need, they had only to knock on the door of the government representative. "Introduced, without being consulted, in the consumer's society, the Eskimo just does that, he consumes," wrote Father Mary and he gave as examples the ever growing sale of carbonated and alcoholic beverages and the introduction of cheap and even pornographic magazines. He could have added the sale of cigarettes. The compulsive tendency to drink pushed some youth to break and enter into the mission during his absence. They opened the safe with a crowbar and stole the mass wine kept inside.

The government had provided the Inuit with regular houses more comfortable than the traditional igloos. The rent was proportional to their income and often their income was negligible. In general, heating, lighting, water supply, and other commodities were free, thus developing a mentality of dependence for those who received direct help. Only the employees drawing substantial wages could buy a skidoo or an A.T.V. (All Terrain Vehicle) and ride about noisily at all hours of the day and night. For the hunters, the situation was not rosy; the price of seal skins had dropped from $30.00 to less than $8.00 because of Brigitte Bardot's ignorant campaign, and of the not less senseless decision of the French government to forbid the importation of skins.

The construction of the Dew Line did not improve the Inuit economy. On the contrary, it turned out to be for many Inuit a traumatic experience. Here is a short extract from *Eskimo*, N. S., N° 12, Fall-Winter 1976-1977: "They (the Inuit) suddenly saw cargo planes land one after the other, letting out tens or hundreds of White men loaded with unimaginable goods. Buildings rose suddenly on the tundra, roads scaled the mountains, flotillas arrived. They also saw expensive machinery abandoned because it would have been more costly to have them repaired than to bring in new ones. They saw bulldozers sometimes crush new material, excellent food thrown in the dump on the pretext that it had been touched by frost or was a bit old...in short, a senseless waste—an example profitable to no one."

His article entitled: *The Missionary... an outcast?* (*Eskimo*, N. S., N° 17, Spring-Summer 1979) won him an appreciation note from W. E. Taylor, the Director of the new Museum of Civilization in Ottawa. Father Mary propounded well the role of the missionary who professes a system of values based on the Gospel in contrast with that of the ethnologist who sometimes goes as far as to consider intolerable all attempts at evangelization.

When ten years later he received an award for his scientific contribution to the North, in his presentation Father Mary stated: "At the time when so many people are criticizing the work of the missionaries and when even some missionaries themselves are expressing doubts about their role and that of their predecessors, I am not going to apologize for the fact that I am a missionary.

Even if the work of missionaries was sometimes too much influenced by their own culture and if there were cases of intolerance and narrow-mindedness, I still believe that by preaching the Gospel we brought to the people a religion of Love to replace the religion of fear that was so vividly described to Knud Rasmussen by the old shaman Aua. At the same time we tried to understand the Inuit and to appreciate their positive values. Some of us have also helped to preserve cultural expressions that had sometimes previously been called pagan rites by others..."

Ottawa—Nanisivik—Pond Inlet

Father Rousselière spent the first months of 1980 in Ottawa, boarding with the Augustinian Fathers in order to be nearer his place of work. Besides analyzing the specimens accumulated during his archaeological discoveries, he wanted to bring the finishing touch to his book *Qitdlarssuaq—L'Histoire d'une migration polaire* (The Story of a Polar Migration) that had been accepted for publication by the University of Montreal. Having read this book, Father Fernand Jetté, Superior General of the Oblates, sent his congratulations from Rome. "This is a fascinating story. I greatly admire the knowledge that you have of the Eskimo world. Such a patient study is surely the irrefutable proof that you love the people!"

At the end of March, on his way to Pond Inlet, he stopped at *Nanisivik* and stayed in the quarters reserved for Anglican and Catholic priests, near the chapel. About 30 people attended Mass. At a temperature of 40° below zero, a truck took him to Arctic Bay where a small house had been built to welcome visiting missionaries. Having plowed into a snow drift, the truck swerved and left the road. They were stuck and had to wait for help.

Nanisivik

Guy Mary-Rousselière travelling to the excavation site

In Arctic Bay, there was only one parishioner, a Jamaican nurse, the Catholic Inuit having all returned home to Igloolik.

During the summer, he continued excavating at *Nunguvik* helped by Susan Rowley and Georgia. The rain was slowing down the digging. At least, they were able to take refuge during the storms in the wood shelter built with Hermann Steltner's help. Hermann was a precious ally for Father Mary. From the Steltners' boat, he recorded the tactics of the killer whale attacking the narwhals. Daily, he was in contact by radio with the "*Polar Continental Shelf Project*", a government organization established at Resolute to assure the logistical support needed by different expeditions in the High Arctic.

At the end of October, in Arctic Bay, Father Mary had just completed a few improvements around the mission when the *Arctic*, an ore tanker built with a reinforced hull, came along on its way to *Nanisivik*. A golden opportunity for Father to visit his parishioners at the mine. For the first time, he was invited to see the whole complex. Millions of years ago, explained the engineer guiding the group, this underground frozen gallery was a cave about three kilometres long which after a while, slowly filled up with zinc and lead sulphides.

In November, at Pelly Bay, Ataata Mari, a few missionaries and several catechists attended a meeting organized by Bishop Robidoux. At the same time, a new chapel was inaugurated replacing the one which had burned down. Father Henry's memory was evidently recalled and also his wish to see one day some Eskimos ordained to the priesthood.

Upon his return to Pond Inlet, for the first time, following a spell of exceptionally mild weather and great velocity winds, he found the sea free of ice, although the winter was already well advanced.

In January 1981, taking advantage of the weekends during another stay at the Museum of Man in Ottawa, he paid a comforting weekly visit to his oldest Inuk parishioner, Solange Atagutsiaq. She had been hospitalized in Montreal with pneumonia. She had lost her right lung and nearly died. However, two months later, she returned to Pond Inlet.

Father Mary's holidays in France, besides his customary visits to Denmark, Holland and Belgium, led him to London to assist at the first communion of a little niece. Then making a detour via Scotland, he stopped at Dundee. In this city's Museum, he was shown a collection of ethnographic discoveries made in 1894 on Somerset Island. The objects were probably coming from the Arctic Bay Eskimos who had disappeared during that period.

On the plane that brought him back to *Nanisivik* at the beginning of July, there were some athletes coming to participate in the Midnight Sun Marathon between Arctic Bay and Nanisivik, about 35 kilometres of up and down trail. By the side of the route, a monument to the memory of Terry Fox had been erected. Father Rousselière was asked to unveil it. The story of Terry Fox, a young Canadian, is well known. After he had a leg amputated, he decided to run across Canada in order to collect money for the fight against cancer. The illness stopped him in Ontario and he died in June. His courage and determination made him a National hero. Even in the North, cancer was taking a heavy toll. Ataata Mari's friend, the old Qumaangapik, his best informer on shamanism, died of lung cancer in May 1981 and in September his widow Inuujaq died of the same illness.

On July 18, Father left by Twin-Otter for *Nunguvik,* accompanied by François de Gerlache, Jean-Louis' brother, and a young man from Ontario, Jean-Paul Isabelle. Jumbo, a big white dog, was also part of the team. One day as Father was digging, he saw from the corner of his eye, a white spot moving. He straightened up ready to shout: "Jumbo" when he found out that it was a powerful white bear passing by, ignoring completely the qallunaat and continuing on his way unperturbed!

15

THE HISTORICAL COMMISSION

Having left Pond Inlet on September 28, on October 3, 1981, Father Rousselière boarded Alitalia and flew to Rome to attend the *Congress on the History and Discovery of the Arctic Regions to the 18th Century*. The Congress was organized by the "Arctic Committee of Monaco." He was not alone to represent Pond Inlet, Sophie Steltner and Desmond Sparham, former local administrator, were also attending. He found there many old acquaintances, Ben Bowditch, an American, who excavated in *Nunguvik* in 1978, J. F. Le Mouël, a Frenchman, who visited Pond Inlet in 1979, just to mention two. Cardinal Garrone opened the Congress by speaking on *"The Role of History and the Classical Disciplines of Man's Development"*. Among the 30 reports presented, that of Father Mary-Rousselière was entitled: *"Exploration and Evangelization of the Great Canadian North: Vikings, Adventurers, Missionaries"*. (*Eskimo* N.S., N° 23, Spring-Summer 1982). The site was magnificent, none other than the Chancellery Palace, but the rest-rooms were rather primitive, he noted with great simplicity! On October 7, members of the Arctic Congress took part at the audience of Pope Jean Paul II who conveyed to them his special greetings. The same day they visited the Vatican library where rare documents on the Arctic had been displayed for their information. In one of his circular letters to his family and friends, he underlined the absence of Malaurie at the Congress in Rome, "he who inexplicably succeeded for 30 years to make himself known in France as THE great specialist on the Eskimos!" "Returning from Rome and its palaces, it feels strange," he wrote Father Jean Drouart whom he called the preaching globe-trotter, "to come back to Canada to discuss wooden huts at a meeting about historical monuments."

In a letter to Bishop Robidoux, written from Pond Inlet on September 14, 1981, he had advised his Bishop that he had become a member of the *"Historic Sites and Monuments Board of Canada"*. His membership was proclaimed on a magnificent document bearing the great seal of Canada with the Queen declaring herself convinced of the fidelity and integrity of her subject, Guy Mary-Rousselière. As representative for the Northwest Territories, he was part of the committee concerned with Native people and fur trading and attended the meeting held on October 18 at the Royal York Hotel in Toronto. The year 1982 witnessed events of great importance for the future of the North. Among them, the referendum on division of the Territories and discussion concerning territorial claims of the Inuit and Dene. Locally, in March, Pond Inlet mourned the death of Solange Atagutsiaq, nicknamed "Sula", a solid Christian and a woman of great influence, crushed by tuberculosis as mentioned previously. Ataata Mari was in Ottawa at the time of her death. Father Lechat flew from Igloolik to Pond Inlet to preside at the funeral of this remarkable lady.

As usual, July was the month to start digging at *Nunguvik*. Susan Scullion, newly graduated from London University in the U.K., and Jean Bracquemond, first president of the court of appeal in Orleans were Father's helpers. Jean Bracquemond, a magistrate fond of sports, had been exploring the rivers of Northern Quebec for many seasons. The previous September at the suggestion of Paul-Emile Victor he had passed through Pond Inlet on his trip around the world via Tahiti and Alaska. He probably had been bitten by the Arctic "bug" to find himself returning to Nunguvik the following summer! Karin Speck and Johannes Heuft, from Germany, were also with the team at the beginning of the excavation. So was a dog named Brownie, spoiled by everybody and much more a house pet than a daring swashbuckler before bears! "We have found once more our old friends", wrote Father Rousselière, "Albert, the seal; Fifi and Lulu, the yellowhammers who came to peck away at our garbage; Daisy, the eider-duck that had feathered its nest at about 30 metres from our working site and has remained faithful; only Aglaë, the ermine did not show up. The bear who took care of our garbage made an appearance but left discreetly when he saw us. The narwhals came as usual and the Inuit hunters killed five of them. The geese arrived in large numbers the day we left for Saatut. There we noticed that the erosion had been particularly heavy this year."

The Great North was a constant source of interest for the media. The film on *Nunguvik* by Thomas Cadieux was presented in February 1982, at the Monte Carlo festival and was an overnight success. T.F.1 in France, showed a film from Radio-Canada on Eskimo archaeology. Better known, the Arctic was attracting more and more scientists and tourists. But, sadly, the real witnesses of the past were disappearing fast. In February, at Iqaluit, Letia Panikpakutsuk died. With her husband and children, she had crossed the North West Passage from east to west on the St. Roch in 1944.

On August 30, 1982, at Nanisivik, Father Rousselière met François Larigas and his wife Martine. They had arrived in the spring by dogsled from Frobisher (Iqaluit).

Their ambition was to reach Anchorage, Alaska, before the beginning of the famous dog race held annually there. Unfortunately, the winter 1982-83 was one of the coldest that the country had known, the thermometer remaining between -40 and -50°C almost constantly from mid-December to April.

Conscious of his pastoral responsibility towards the community of *Nanisivik*, Father Mary tried to visit there once a month. This was a costly deal, plane tickets being very expensive. In March 1982, Radio-France offered him a free trip. He accepted and found as guests of the mine a team of "France-Inter" who had landed there to monitor the expedition of Janusc Kurbiel to the Magnetic Pole by skidoo. He was himself interviewed by Jacques Pradel, an interview that was telecast in France a few weeks later. At *Nanisivik*, he also met a French military detachment from Chamonix on its way to Bylot. To facilitate their march, he offered them the hospitality of the old mission at Pond Inlet, which for a month was transformed into a military barrack. Commandant Marmier and his men arrived there by skidoo and then crossed the sea toward Bylot, travelling through the glaciers, climbing the highest peaks and all this by 47°C below zero weather. Finally, on April 24, a French military plane came to repatriate everybody. To show their gratitude to Father Rousselière, they left him a few delicacies such as truffled liver pâté, a Saint Emilion, and even prunes à l'Armagnac. A heaven-sent gift enabling him to welcome with dignity Bishop Robidoux who, on May 9, landed at Pond Inlet. After meeting the Inuit, the Bishop proceeded to the confirmation service. Late in the evening, when left alone, Father Mary discussed with him the financial situation of *Eskimo* magazine. He judiciously brought to his attention that it would not be exaggerated to raise the price of subscription to $2.00, "considering the price of carrots at Pond Inlet"! He also told the Bishop that he would like to see the publication of a new Prayer Book using the new spelling and brought up to date with the new liturgy. The text was being revised by Father Théophile Didier, an expert in Inuktitut language whose translation of the Old Testament proved to be a great success even among Anglicans. As for the presentation of this new Prayer Book, he recommended putting face to face the syllabic and Roman orthographies. A great scholar, Father Mary kept himself informed on the evolution in the Church and the revision to Canon Law.

May-June 1993, he was in Montreal to see his doctor, then in Quebec, to take part in the meeting of the Historic Sites and Monuments Board. In summer, at *Nanisivik,* he registered for the famous mini-marathon of the Midnight Sun (10 kilometres) and in spite of a sciatic attack, he won the "zinc" medal!

Due to a scholarship extended by the "Young Explorers Club" of New York to honour his archaeological achievements, he welcomed to help him in the July digging at *Saatut* and *Nunguvik*, his little niece Carolyne Timberlake of England and her friend Sarah Lord. Both seventeen years old, came bubbling over with enthusiasm and, more important, with a keen sense of observation. They were given the chance to see "Cleopatra", the big whale that stayed a few days in the vicinity and also "Ursula" the mother lemming who with her son, the small "Zephirin" dug their burrow together. The number of people interested by Father Mary-Rousselière's research increased year by year. Clermont and Danielle Guay of *Nanisivik* and their two children joined them for a few days. Tourists, piloted by Graham and Diana Rowley, came ashore from the *Lindblad Explorer* to inspect the excavation site. The next day, August 19, the site was closed.

During his sojourn in Europe, September-October 1983, besides the pleasure of seeing his family and visiting his friends at the four corners of the continent, he presented the film on *Nunguvik* at the Copenhagen Museum, at St. Martin de Pontoise College and at the Geographic Society of Paris. This was the same room where the distribution of prizes was held when he attended Fontanes School, and where Father Petitot had spoken of his Arctic Coast discoveries about a hundred years ago. Attractive invitations sent by his friend Jean-François Le Mouël brought an audience that filled the room. The evening ended in the most appropriate way with a visit to the *Procope,* the oldest café, a landmark of Paris.

Back in Canada on October 17, he arrived at Pond Inlet on the 26th, delayed at *Nanisivik* by zero visibility and a blizzard so violent that it tore to pieces the roof of the mine. Barely settled for winter, he went again south November 15 until December 1st. During his absence, the alarm system, recently installed in the mission, went off and woke up neighbours who understood that the mission furnace had stopped!

Germany

June 1984, Father Mary-Rousselière responded to an invitation to attend a seminar on the Arctic in Bamberg, Germany. It was organized by Professors Erhard Treude and Hansjurgen Müller-Beck. On May 30, with his superior's permission and all expenses paid by the German government, he left Canada and went to Nuremberg via Frankfurt where Jean-Loup Rousselot, a French ethnologist he had met in Rome was waiting for him. At Bamberg, he gave a lecture on the *"Factors that Influence the Human Occupation in the Region of Pond Inlet from the*

Prehistoric Era until Today. " Bamberg is a beautiful small city filled with historical monuments, among which, at the Cathedral, the tomb of Emperor St. Henri and of St. Cunégonde, his wife and also the tomb of the only German Pope, Clement II. Father Mary's sense of humour was always vivid. After his visit to the Cathedral, he sent to Bishop Robidoux, a card representing a portion of the last judgement where among the damned could be clearly seen a mitre and he added, "I regret but there were no bishops on the side showing the Chosen!" When in Bavaria, he admitted that he had never drunk so many different kinds of beer but never beyond the limits of ecclesiastical decorum!

After Bamberg, together with about 20 participants of the seminar, he visited Tubingen, a picturesque city of about 70, 000 souls, half of whom were students. In Tubingen, they held a meeting in the large Schloss tower, the medieval château that shelters the Anthropological and Archaeological Departments of the University.

June 6, he arrived back in Canada. On the 12th, he attended a meeting of the Historic Sites and Monuments held at the Francophone University of Moncton in New Brunswick. He noticed how Acadians and Québécois differ in many ways. They use very different expressions of speech and have their own flag, the French flag with a star as a symbol of the Holy Virgin Mary. In this coastal country, they were offered a lobster dinner in the little village of Cocagne. Later, by bus, they visited Fort Beausejour, a former French Fort, well restored, then via Sackville and the Anglophone University of Mount Allison, late in the evening, they reached St. John, in the Bay of Fundy.

July 10, Father Rousselière was again at *Nunguvik*, this time with three Canadian students and the faithful Brownie who had the mandate to warn the camp that King Nanuk was approaching. The geese were plentiful. On the night preceding their departure from the site, a fox succeeded in catching a goose before it could reach the water but, pursued by the young excavators, it let it go and with tail at low mast, ran to its burrow. The goose was eaten the next day at Pond Inlet in the company of Don and Katy Lou McLauchlan, two old friends of the R.C.M.P. he had known at Baker Lake and who were now travelling as tourists discovering a new part of the Arctic.

On June 29, Ataata Mary noted that it had been 40 years, to the day, since he had arrived at Pond Inlet on the *Nascopie*. The village counted only a few houses then and many igloos. Now septuagenarian, he was still in good health. A bit austere at first, he had in reality a very warm and compassionate heart. Sensitive to the sorrows of others, he wanted to express all his sympathy to Bishop Robidoux who had just lost his sister. His thoughts were often with the members of his family stricken by illness or old age and he carried them all in his prayers.

In September 1984, he would have loved to attend Pope John Paul II's visit to Canada with his confrères and some Inuit from Igloolik who went to Winnipeg to greet the *"Isirardjuarapik"*, the great, great priest. The flight schedule and the fog did not allow him to do so. He watched the magnificent event on TV, listening to the Pope's speeches and looking at the marching crowd. The problems concerning the Church as much as the future of the Inuit never ceased to preoccupy him. His article entitled: *"Inculturation? Yes but Where to Stop?"* published in the *Kerygma* magazine (N° 19, 1985) shows a well informed, critical mind. In a letter to Father Jean Drouart, he admitted having been passive too long regarding the points of contention in the Church but that from now on he had decided to fight, and if need be, to stir up a little scandal!

At the end of November, a team from Los Angeles arrived to interview him and film what was of interest around Pond Inlet in spite of the lack of exterior light. "I'm beginning to have the impression," he wrote to his family, "that I am considered somewhat a curiosity of the Panda type or a calf with six legs!"

He was considered a man of great knowledge. In the latest volume of the Smithsonian Institution's Handbook of North American Indians, he had been invited to make a contribution to this scholarly overview of Arctic culture relating to the Igloolik Eskimos.

When describing leadership he wrote: "The camp usually had a leader or Isumataq. A large village might have several men so designated. He was generally a mature and experienced man, who was a good hunter and the head of a large family. The function of the Isumataq and the shaman were often combined. Except in the case of outstanding personalities, the Isumataq was rather the first among equals, and only after consulting the other heads of families did he proceed to coordinate the activities, divide tasks, and sometimes distribute the game."

In another excerpt, he described the notion of a soul as fundamental to the religious beliefs of the Iglulik Eskimo. "All that exists has a soul or can have one. Man has a double soul: inusiq, the breath of life, and tarniq, the soul proper. One's name, atiq, is also a kind of soul, generally inherited from an ancestor. The soul of an animal that was killed takes over a new body, hence the necessity not to offend it. One legend shows a human soul reincarnated in a series of animal forms, and finally in the form of a man. Sickness comes from the loss of a soul or part of it, which may have been stolen."

In December 1984, the Research Group on Arctic Ecology welcomed him at Strasbourg for a session entitled "*The Polar Night*" with all expenses paid by the Director General of the Cultural Affairs Department in Ottawa. December 21st, at the request of His Excellency, the Consul of Canada, he gave a presentation to the representatives of diverse travel agencies, hoping to convince them that Pond Inlet and Nanisivik could attract tourists as well as Costa Brava! The next day, he and Robert Gessain, Honourary Director of the Museum of Man in Paris, presided at a dinner debate on the Canadian North that lasted well after midnight. He presented films on the "*Netjilit*" showing the inseparable interaction between man and ice! Above all, he rejoiced to spend Christmas with his family, only the second time since 1933. The only shadow to his joy was to learn that Pond Inlet was without a priest on that day and that his Mass wine had again been stolen!

Pond Inlet—Ottawa—France

Father Rousselière landed in Pond Inlet the first of January 1985. If he did avoid the cold spell that hit Europe that year, he did not escape a minus 40 to minus 50 temperature in Mittimatalik during February. Of course, the Inuit are used to facing cold weather and Europeans are not.

In March 1985, Dr. Louis Richard, a Corsican doctor and his wife, an elderly couple coming straight from Sari d'Orcino knocked at Father Mary's door. Dr. Richard had known Arsène Turquetil, the founder of the Central Eskimo Missions, in the little Seminary in France, a coincidence which from the start gave a friendly atmosphere to their encounter.

In May 1985, the Oblates of the Hudson Bay Diocese had their pastoral meeting in Ottawa and their annual retreat in Orleans animated by Father Léon Van Hoorde, the well-known apostle of "La Poudrière" in Brussels. Father Rousselière joined them a few days later. He did compensate however his delay in reading Father Martelet's book "*2000 Ans d'Église en Question*". "A book that was better", he wrote, "than all the study sessions given on new ministries and the communautés de base."

Having been kept south for medical checkups, it was only on July 8 that he flew back to Pond Inlet together with his excavating companions, both from overseas, Jacques Martin, director of a school for the professional development of adults in Chambery and Hélène de Gerlache, a registered nurse, the sister of Jean-Louis and François.

On July 11, they left by plane for *Nunguvik,* favoured by exceptionally fair weather and, as a ransom for this hot spell, millions of mosquitoes attacking from all sides. However, the use of repellent lotions or mosquito-netting allowed the excavations to go on. One night, a bear came close to the camp but was routed away by the barking of the intrepid Brownie. Its bravery won him the name "The Lion of Nunguvik"!

The research team arrived back at Pond Inlet on August 15, pleased with their discoveries: a small mephistophelean head carved in wood whose horns were made of two little branches, two small masks, one in antler, located by Jacques in the *Arnakadlak* site, dating probably many centuries before Christ and one in ivory found at *Nunguvik* by Helène de Gerlache.

A month later, Father Rousselière was in France, on his way to Mullem, Belgium, having been invited to assist at the wedding of Henrianne de Gerlache, Hélène's sister.

The mass was celebrated in Flemish in a magificently restored church endowed with a 12th century tower.

In Orleans, about one hundred kilometres south of Paris, he visited Jean Bracquemond who had been at Pond Inlet three consecutive years and had promised himself that he would return again in 1984 and 1985. But his health failed him and he died not long after, deeply missed by all the friends that his enthusiasm and his good humour had won him in the North.

On October 17, Father Mary celebrated his 50th religious anniversary with a few confrères at Fontenay-sous-Bois, east of Paris, and three days later, he was on his way to Canada and more precisely to Mittimatalik. During his absence, the northern desert had been swept by violent storms, tearing off roofs, stopping planes from landing and accumulating ice on the shore to the extent that all travel by skidoo became difficult.

Pond Inlet not only had its nursing station, its Post Office, but also its hotel made of eleven units built in the South by ATCO, transported by ship in September and assembled by white and local workers equipped with regular boots and helmets. The hotel offered all the modern comforts with a bathroom in each room and cleaning staff in uniform. It was officially inaugurated on the 4th of December, Ataata Mari blessing the building and the oldest lady of the settlement cutting the traditional ribbon—in this instance, a strip of seal skin—with her *ulu*. The full per day rate at the *Sauniq Hotel* was set at $150.

The year 1986 was rich in activities for the Arctic Research Establishment (ARE) directed by his friend Hermann Steltner. Four groups of young Inuit from Baffin Land received on the premises a scientific and technical initiation with the last day of their training reserved for an outline on archaeology and traditional culture given by Father Rousselière. A local dramatic art troupe came to consult Ataata Mari about a new play in Inuktitut and English depicting the ancestral life and its evolution. In June, he spoke on the history and prehistory of the country to some ornithologists from Ottawa, interested in Arctic birds.

Delayed by snow and ice, it was only on the 6th of July that he landed in *Nunguvik,* together with Mary-Pat Short, a Nanisivik teacher and his old friend Ed Jordan from Ottawa.

The weather stayed so cold that the mosquitoes did not dare show up. The digging lasted to the end of July and kept Father Mary physically in good shape; he did not even complain of the usual shoulder ache recurring every summer since his skidoo accident in 1963; it stopped as if by magic, without any injections of cortisone.

All summer long, the weather was miserable. However, on the 29th of August, the *World Explorer* anchored in Pond Inlet with some tourists accompanied by Dr. Moreau S. Maxwell[1], a great American archaeologist well known to Father Rousselière who was unfortunately away in Winnipeg at the time of the ship's visit.

In fall, the weather improved a great deal and the sea was so calm that on the 15th of October it was entirely frozen over, indeed a very rare phenomenon. It did not prevent an ice-breaker showing up in the open sea ten kilometres away, apparently on the look-out for a boat it had been requested to escort. At night, its lights were visible until the 26th of November.

---

[1] Cf. *Prehistory of the Eastern Arctic* by Moreau S. Maxwell, Department of Anthropology, Michigan State University, East Lansing, Michigan, USA, (1985).

16

TRAGEDY AT RANKIN INLET

The year 1986 ended by a tragedy affecting the whole Hudson Bay Diocese. Bishop Robidoux, Father Didier and Sister Lise Turcotte s.g.m., perished in a plane crash at Rankin Inlet on November 12. Father Mary-Rousselière was deeply saddened by this sudden loss of people dear to him. He appreciated Bishop Robidoux very much for his dynamism, his unique way of encouraging the initiatives of his missionaries, his zeal for the formation of native catechists and his preoccupation towards strong and faithful Inuit families. He was also full of esteem for Father Didier, a great intellectual and an unrepentant absent-minded man like himself! Father Didier was almost irreplaceable as translator of the Bible and other liturgical texts, being an expert in the Eskimo language as well as in Hebrew and Greek. For Father Mary, he was an old friend. Sister Lise also was loved and respected as a catechetical specialist, always bringing new ideas but also a communicative joy and optimism. The night before the disaster, Father Mary had landed at Pelly Bay and with a few other Oblates already there, was waiting for the plane from Churchill coming via Rankin. No plane came! A message bringing the tragic news of the accident spread consternation in the whole community. The small two-engine Navajo plane had crashed a short distance from the runway after an unsuccessful take-off. Bouncing on the rocks, it had caught fire, throwing in the night a sinister flame which reduced everything and everyone to ashes. *"Remember, Ô man, that you are dust!"* "Where others see an absurdity, we see a mystery", wrote Father Rousselière.

On November 19, what would have been Bishop Robidoux's 73rd birthday, Father Mary attended the funeral for the victims of the crash. The ceremony took place in St. Boniface Cathedral. The three very simple coffins of wood covered with grey flannel, containing the calcinated remains of the Bishop, the Priest and the Sister were placed side by side in front of the altar.

As if to add to the gloom of the day, news arrived from Rankin Inlet that, the night of the accident, Father Lorson, in charge of Our Lady of the Cape Mission, was found unconscious, struck down by a brain tumor. Brought to St. Boniface hospital, he was successfully operated on. And as if the sky was still not gray enough and the feeling of emptiness not bitter enough, Ataata Mari saw Father Vandevelde permanently leaving the North to retire in Belgium. After 50 years in the Arctic, Ataata Vinivi was suffering from arthritis of the hip and had a hearing problem making his ministry difficult.

Father Mary's family was not spared from death of relatives and friends, even people of his own age. He himself was often asked when he would retire, a question he would not answer but that brought home the implacable fact that he was aging also! Notwithstanding his 73 years of age and 48 years of missionary life, he was still perfectly lucid.

He was, intellectually speaking, at the very top of his career. Always fond of reading, he enjoyed particularly the books dealing with the Church. Like John the XXIII, he agreed that the windows should be opened to let fresh air come in... but without throwing out the furniture any more than the prescriptions of Canon Law! He regretted that along with the term "People of God", the expression "Body of Christ" had not been preserved and also that the hierarchical Church appeared too often like a scarecrow wearing the mask of Cardinal Ratzinger, the author of *Talks on Faith*, a book that he found very objective, but, he added, "was it a sign of his own mental deficiency?" He did not think so. He knew he was in agreement with Cardinal de Lubac, Ur Von Balthasar and other Church leaders, even protestant ones such as the Lutheran theologian G. Dreyfus, Director of the Centre of European Studies at Strasbourg University. In an article expressing his opinions on Vatican II, twenty years later, Dr. Dreyfus spoke of the Zwinglian skid of the Church of France. Father Rousselière agreed.

He worried about the shortage of priestly vocations and probably more so about the actual role of the priest "who only has to back up graciously after giving over to the laity all the tasks that he had assumed until now." Nevertheless, he remained optimistic, following John Paul II for whom "nothing can be substituted to the ordained ministry". The more balanced attitude of at least a part of the young clergy was for him a ray of hope.

On January 15, 1987, he went to Churchill to see to the affairs of *Eskimo* magazine and also to meet Brother Volant, curator of the Eskimo Museum and his assistant, Lorraine Brandson with whom he wished to fully co-operate in the classification of archaeological collections and photographic archives of the Diocese.

From Churchill, he headed for St. Catharines. After a day of relaxation at Niagara Falls, his friend Hermann Steltner initiated him in the use of the computer. Father had decided to enter the age of electronic information,

283

probably somewhat presumptuous on his part to try competing with his grand-nephews and nieces!

Two weeks later, I greeted him at the Ottawa airport and for the next few days made myself his benevolent chauffeur, driving him to the Asticou Complex in Hull where the Museum of Man had offices and collections of specimens in reserve.

Dr. Bryan Gordon, a friend and archaeologist described the contribution of Father Rousselière to the National Museum in these terms: "Never have I seen such wonderful art and tools brought to the National Museum in Ottawa (now the Canadian Museum of Civilization) on such a shoestring budget. Each year I marvelled at his newest finds fresh from his black attaché case: miniature tools, menacing shamanistic figures and articulated dolls of wood. One year I saw a model of the earliest known skis of the Canadian Arctic."

Concerning the personality of Father Rousselière, Dr. Gordon wrote: "Seemingly aloof and reserved to some, perhaps a result of his habituation in lonely settlements, he was warm, generous, frugal with field funds, fair to all, introspective but also ready to enjoy a joke. For those of us who work in the Arctic, he was a colleague and a friend."

After work, he often asked to be taken to the homes of northern friends, the Rowleys, the McLauchlans, etc. One morning, he sat in the car and as usual had difficulty buckling his seat belt. After finally succeeding, he said to me: "Today, I will photograph a few artifacts". Then, a couple minutes later as we were already in the centre of the City of Ottawa: "Zut! I forgot my camera". His absent-mindedness, though at times embarrassing, made him very likeable.

On February 26, back at Pond Inlet, he welcomed the members of an expedition that came from Igloolik by dogsled on its way to Greenland in the footsteps of Qitdlarssuaq. This Eskimo ancestor had made the trip around 1850, as reported in the book Father Rousselière had written titled *"A Story of a Polar Migration"*.

Around that same time, he received an invitation from Paul-Emile Victor to meet him at Eureka where Victor was giving a helping hand to Hubert de Chevigny and Nicholas Hulot in their successful attempt to the North Pole. Eureka being 800 kilometres from Pond Inlet, Father Mary declined.

From July 9 to August 10, he spent a month at the excavating site of *Nunguvik* with a young student from Ottawa, Christopher, the son of his friends John and Colly Scullion and a young French lady, Monique Daniel, professor of geography at Chambery and an experienced sportwoman. A few geese flapping their wings landed near the site. Thinking that a roasted goose would be a pleasant change from the habitual preserves, Father Rousselière had bought a hunting licence but seeing that he could approach the gaggling birds without scaring them away, rifle in hand, he did not have the heart to shoot! "Truly", he concluded, "I do not have the guts of an Eskimo!"

Four days after the beginning of the excavations, Daniel, one of his parishioners and the 21 year old son of Alain Maktar, drowned accidentally at Pond Inlet. The helicopter of the "Polar Continental Shelf Project" came to pick up Ataata Mari to preside at the funeral.

Bishop Rouleau

On July 29, 1987, Reynald Rouleau, Provincial of Our Lady of the Rosary Oblate province at Quebec, was ordained Bishop of the Churchill-Hudson Bay Diocese in Rankin.

Therese Maktar and her son Daniel

Father Rousselière put himself immediately and entirely at his service "as long as God keeps him healthy." He loved to say that, among his confrères, he represented the tendency "obedience to the Pope" before any other consideration. He had followed the conciliar liturgy as well as the pastoral suggestions that had been given to the missionaries. Concerning his attitude, he wrote: "If some find me a bit behind times and raising too many objections to novelties, I have nevertheless no reason to believe that I have to be considered as senile." He had not attended the Oblate session that year in Ottawa, because the main topic of discussion regarding morality was presented by André Guindon, controversial professor at St. Paul University, much too avant-gardiste to his liking!

Reflecting on his long stay at Pond Inlet, Father Mary agreed that the small number of Catholics did not justify the presence in the settlement of a priest who had no other interest than the pastoral ministry. Of course, he was a priest looking after his parishioners, but he was also a researcher, a scientist and as such, he was hoping to spend the next two years preparing his final archaeological report. A task which had become easier since he was now equipped with a Tandy computer and even a printer purchased with a thousand dollar grant from the Social Sciences and Humanities Research Council of Canada.

In August, the boat brought Father Rousselière some material to insulate his house. The furnace could no longer heat it satisfactorily, the wind penetrating from everywhere. To do the work alone would have been for him an impossible task but under the supervision of Hermann Steltner and the help of some Inuit, the work was completed before winter. Hermann was not living in Pond Inlet anymore but each summer, he remained a faithful visitor, following closely the work of the "Arctic Research Establishment"

Guy Mary-Rousselière and Bishop Rouleau with two candidates for confirmation—Pond Inlet

and devoting his free time to the mission. After the death of Bishop Robidoux, he generously initiated the Bishop Robidoux Foundation for the education of young Inuit.

On September 20, the day Alain Maktar represented Pond Inlet at the Pope's visit to Fort Simpson, Father Rousselière arrived in Paris. "My vacation is hectic as usual", he wrote. In Belgium after blessing the marriage of François de Gerlache and Isabelle, he went to visit Father Vandevelde who was pleased to welcome him in his new retirement home, his "*Nutkrarvikulu*". Then he took the train to Copenhagen where he spent an evening at Jørgen Meldgaard's home with Eigil Knuth. Famous anthropologist, Eigil Knuth had crossed Greenland in 1936, with Victor, Gessain and Perez. Last summer, he had celebrated his 83rd anniversary excavating in the extreme north of Greenland. In London, Father visited again the British Museum. He was shown objects brought from Igloolik by Parry in 1823, even well preserved caribou-skin clothing. In the Museum, an exhibition on the Great Canadian North was attracting many tourists. Its main goal was to prove that hunting and trapping were the two basic pillars of the traditional native way of life, in opposition to the current propaganda against the fur trade which was so detrimental to the Inuit.

Bishop Rouleau was due in Pond Inlet to celebrate on December 17, 1987, the 50th anniversary of Father Mary's ordination. But the North being the country of the unexpected, Monseigneur arrived only on January 4, coming from Nanisivik. He brought with him a miner's lamp made of copper, engraved with Father Rousselière's name, a gift from the Mine personnel sent to their visiting missionary on his jubilee. Receiving with emotion this very special sign of esteem from the Nanisivik people, he said with a smile: "It will replace my old Aladdin lamp in case of black-out!" Alain Maktar on his part contributed to the banquet marking the Bishop's visit and the Father's jubilee by bringing a large piece of caribou and frozen arctic char.

On February 5, 1988, Father Rousselière flew south again to be operated on for a hernia. He spent his convalescence at the Oblate Monastery in Richelieu before returning north on March 2. On the morning of March 18th, Rebecca, a young Inuk schoolteacher, was found frozen to death on the side of the road, her clothing torn and her body partly eaten by the dogs. Once more, it seemed, alcohol was the culprit.

On April 25, a group of Greenlanders arrived by plane from Qânaq, staying at Pond Inlet for a week, a worthy continuation to the exchange of people started by Father Rousselière in 1972.

In May 1988, all the Oblates of the North were invited to take part to the International Oblate Pilgrimage, held under the protection of Our Lady at Cap-de-la-Madeleine. Father Rousselière, like all the members of the Arctic group, was easily recognizable by his white anorak with its pointed hood and the crest of the diocese sewn on the front. Even former northern missionaries each received an anorak as a sign of gratitude for the years spent working with the Inuit. Among them, Fathers Steinmann, Ferron, and Trinel, all three retired in the Monastery of Our Lady of the Cape, also Father Haramburu who had come from Nice. During the Congress, Father Marcello Zago, the Superior General, paid the Northern missionaries a very stimulating visit and gave to all the participants a presentation on the place of Mary in the Oblate spirituality.

Nicolet, the town from which the Grey Nuns left for Chesterfield in 1931, is not very far from Cap-de-la-Madeleine. It was just proper for the Oblates who had

Guy Mary-Rousselière—Cap-de-la-Madeleine (1988)

known and appreciated the Sisters in the North to go and greet their former co-workers in the apostolate of the Hudson Bay. The Sisters were delighted to see them and to talk about the Inuit to whom they had devoted their lives.

The 22nd of May was a Sunday. The fog was extremely dense and the driving hazardous. However, all arrived safe and on time at St. Pascal-Baylon (Wendover) for the early morning mass presided by Monseigneur Rouleau and during which he performed the missionary send-off of Lynne Rollin, a young local girl who had accepted to serve the Church among the Inuit for a five year period together with Joanne Dionne of Portage La Prairie, Manitoba. Father Rousselière pointed out how encouraging it was to see young women and men giving the best years of their lives to make Christ and His Message better known.

After a few days spent in Ottawa at the Museum, he returned home to Pond Inlet on June 4th. He was surprised to see that almost all the snow had disappeared and that habitual summer visitors were already arriving. The first being Hermann and Sophie Steltner, always delighted in seeing again their Inuit friends. They were accompanied by some scientists anxious to spend a few weeks on Bylot Island looking for dinosaur bones. Some bones had been discovered the summer before, dating back to more than 60 million years. Among the researchers, most of them geologists, was Dr. Dale Russell, from the Division of Vertebrates at the National Museum.

On the 16th of July, four people arrived from Lyon, France, and found hospitality in the old mission. They had planned to follow the coast by kayak to Clyde River and to film, for France 2, different scenes on the ice but, alas, a very unsual happening, all the ice had gone south or had melted!

Taking advantage of the nice weather, Father Rousselière completed the insulation of the mission's walls, under Hermann's supervision and with the help of some local prisoners sentenced to community work by way of punishment. He also welcomed John Bockstoce, an explorer, Curator of the Ethnology Section at the Whaling Museum in Bedford, Massachussets, who arrived from Alaska on the "Belvedere", an 18 metre motor boat. In his free time, Father Mary read with interest Bockstoce's book on "Whales and Whalers of the West Arctic".

On Sunday September 4, 1988, the NWT commissioner, John Parker, passed through Pond Inlet and invited Father Rousselière for dinner at *Sauniq*, the local hotel. Commissioner Parker was accompanied by members of the Canada Arts Council and its President, the renowned Canadian singer, Maureen Forrester. Father Rousselière greeted Ms. Forrester and informed her of the limited range of music that was broadcast in the North, predominantly Rock'n roll.

In October 4, another gala dinner at the hotel in honour of Sophie and Hermann Steltner. Hermann had donated the ARE laboratory and its equipment to the hamlet of Mittimatalik. He received in exchange a magnificent soapstone sculpture, a gift he would always cherish as a souvenir of the Inuit he had known so well. Their departure left a feeling of sadness for many people in the village, a sadness increased by a heavy snowfall and orchestrated by the dismal cawing of a few raven. For Ataata Mari, the raven was one of the most congenial birds in the North. "It has no hair on its legs as does the ptarmigan, does not disguise itself in white as the arctic hare does and always plays the fool."

17

THE NORTHERN SCIENCE AWARD

The Northern Science Award had been inaugurated in 1982-83, during the International Polar Year and awarded usually to renowned university researchers from the South. It was time to choose a laureate from the Arctic. The Canadian Government decided that Father Mary-Rousselière was the best candidate for this prestigious award for the year 1988.

On January 19, 1989, the Honourable Bill McKnight, Minister of Indian and Northern Affairs, presented him with a large silver medal and a substantial cheque. The presentation took place in one of the most beautiful rooms of the Parliament Buildings. In his answer to many very touching speeches, Father underlined the fact that he was receiving this honour in the name of all the Oblate missionaries who had devoted themselves to the service of the Inuit in the North. He also mentioned the Inuit who had with competence and faithfulness helped him in his research and especially the late Bernard Iqugaqtuq of Pelly Bay. For their benefit, he ended his speech with a brief message in Inuktitut. The offical ceremony attended by Monseigneur Rouleau, Father Vandevelde, Alain Maktar, the Scullions and many more friends was followed by a marvelous banquet in the Lester B. Pearson Building, accompanied by a delicious

Presentation of the Northern Science Award (Ottawa, January 1989)

Châteauneuf-du-Pape! Pond Inlet having become a mini-metropolis with one thousand inhabitants, could be proud of its missionary, no less than the Congregation of the Oblates.

In a letter to the laureate, the Superior General Father Marcello Zago wrote this: "Through your love for the Inuit,...., you were always ready to listen attentively and methodically to the voice of their culture. You became an anthropologist and an archaeologist, desirous to link and to understand the present and the past of the North. Your works and their conclusions show us a people whose odyssey recalls the advance of the People of Israel in the desert among difficulties of all kind, difficulties that finally gave it its identity."

But soon the rejoicing surrounding the award came to an end. Eight days later, Father Mary was on the operating table for another hernia. After a convalescence at Richelieu, he returned to Pond Inlet on February 20.

On May 16, he left for St. Boniface where the annual retreat was held. On June 2, he went to Edmonton for the diocesan meeting held at the Grey Nuns Centre, headed by Bishop Rouleau. Father Rousselière did not miss the opportunity to insist that all priests should obey the rubrics concerning the celebration of the Mass. "Truly, if we are convinced that we are renewing the sacrifice of the Cross, I do not see how we can partake of it as if we were going to have a drink with a friend at the corner pub. The praxis must be the reflection of the faith", he wrote with the conviction of one who is first a priest and is not always in agreement with everyone and anyone. And aiming at those who neglected the application of the Canons concerning the liturgy, he added with a certain sarcasm: "Evidently if some of us are dispensed from the observation of Canon Law by a direct intervention from the Holy Spirit, I bow to them with a respectful admiration!"

Back at Pond Inlet on June 12, Father Rousselière found the village half empty. As soon as school closed, the Inuit left for their summer camps to go hunting. On the 15th, he welcomed his cousins Yvette and George Bertrand who enjoyed the midnight sun for a whole week but, to Father Guy's regret, did not have a chance to go for a dogteam ride. The ice was not safe any more.

In July, his friends John and Colly Scullion and François Bottini, a Parisian student, spent several days preparing and packing for the expedition to Nunguvik and Arnakadlak. Tents had to be repaired, lists of supplies had to be prepared and countless items had to be located. This was not an easy task in a place like Pond Inlet!

The day of the big move to camp another major problem arose! As the plane approached to land on the primitive airstrip close to the *Nunguvik* site, the pilot could see a stream dissecting the strip in two! It was not possible to land there, so an alternative gravel beach was found some three kilometres away!

The mountain of gear and supplies had to be ferried on foot or by ATV (all terrain vehicle) to the *Nunguvik* site. Father Rousselière was completely business like and calmly dealt with all the extra work entailed. In true Inuit fashion, he adjusted to all the frustrations that the land, nature and the weather dealt the expedition.

Nunguvik camp life was finally set up; it was very orderly, disciplined and professional. Daily routines and schedules for work and cooking meals were clearly defined and all major chores were shared. Water patrol had to trudge to the airstrip stream and keep the water containers full.

The airstrip had to be hand groomed and ready all the time to accept an emergency landing by a *Twin Otter*.

The focus of the camp was always on the "dig". Father Mary trained his friends well and always communicated and shared his great knowledge and skills. Excavation work went on six days a week in all weather. The evening meal was followed by long discussions on far ranging topics. It was an exhausting pace that Father Rousselière set for himself and his friends but always sparkled by good humour and joy in the task at hand. In this close intimate setting, the group became a "family" living in harmony, sharing and working hard together to explore the Inuit past.

Father Mary loved to prepare the morning porridge; it was sometimes very wet like soup and other times like glue that refused to leave the bowl or spoon! He always prepared extra for Brownie, the pampered guard dog. Father would beat an empty oil drum with a large caribou bone to advise the camp that breakfast was imminent. To add a challenge to daily life, he would beat out the tune of a song and the campers were expected to solve the puzzle! The repertoire was always original and included such tunes as "O Canada", "Pack up your Troubles", "Rule Britannia" "La Marseillaise" and church hymns.

On August 4, the "*World Discoverer*", a luxurious cruiser, arrived at *Nunguvik*. A flotilla of zodiacs brought 120 tourists ashore. They were mostly German and American, under Dr. Moreau S. Maxwell's mentorship as the year before. Father Mary-Rousselière gave them a warm welcome as he had done a few days earlier to Hermann Steltner and to Dr. Dale Russell. Dr. Russell had landed in Pond Inlet in order to continue his research on the dinosaurs of Bylot Island. He was accompanied by Dr. Dong Zhiming, a Chinese archaeologist who had just returned from

Europe and was very interested in the physical resemblances between the Chinese and Eskimos.

Two days later, the usual scenario, a white bear came close to the camp but did not dare enter because of the protesting bark of Brownie. Hungry, he satisfied himself pilfering the boxes of spaghetti and the bags of flour piled up at the end of the runway. Father, after making sure that the bear was not around anymore, went to repair the mess, saving what he could. A little later, Colly Scullion who was then alone in the tent came out and had the surprise of her life finding herself face to face with the bear. She addressed Nanuk with such strong invectives that the king of the tundra fled and threw itself into the sea!

On September 10, tireless globe-trotter, Father Mary-Rousselière landed at Orly. He did not mind flying but still liked travelling by train better, more so now that the TGV[1] seemed to have abolished distances. Le Mans, his native city, was only 55 minutes from Paris. He arrived there, October 15, in time to celebrate Mass at the cathedral on the occasion of a special missionary day. Back in Paris, he met Paul-Emile Victor who had just published, fifty years after his stay in Ammassalik, a book entitled: *La Civilisation du Phoque (The Civilization of the Seal)*, the account of his ethnographic studies. According to Father Mary, the great explorer told him when they parted: "I envy you your belief in another world. As for myself, I can only hope."

Ataata Mari returned to Canada at the end of October. After visiting the Museum of Civilization in Ottawa, the new museum whose name he accepted with a slight reticence, the name "Museum of Man" being according to him more appropriate, he went to Winnipeg. He wanted to

---

[1] T.G.V.: Train à Grande Vitesse or the train travelling at great speed.

find an editor[2] for the English version of his book on the Migration to Greenland, translated from the French by Alan Cooke. Alan had died in July 1989, and Father Mary had not been informed of his death.

From Winnipeg, he went to Battleford where the "Marian Press" owned by the Oblates, prints, with much expertise but too often with some delay, the ESKIMO Magazine. Then via Toronto, St. Catharines and *Nanisivik*, he returned to Pond Inlet on February 1, 1990.

April 17, arriving from *Nanisivik* where he had celebrated Easter, Monseigneur Rouleau came to celebrate Confirmation at Pond Inlet. The following day, a team from French Television arrived unexpectedly. For four days, the cameramen were busy filming Father Mary-Rousselière. One day, Ataata Mary had to travel by dogteam with an Eskimo, both of course clad in caribou fur. The Inuk had a good *koliktar,* light and warm. Father had borrowed one from the police, stiff as cardboard and open in front, ill protecting him from the cold. Suddenly, the dogs made a bolt for what they probably thought was a seal on the ice and the sled violently struck a block of ice. Father, half frozen, was graciously ejected from the sled to find himself face first in the snow. Standing up, he started looking everywhere for his glasses when someone told him that they were still sitting on his nose! All he got out of this incident was a bad cold.

May 1, the same French Television team came back from Resolute with two balloons and a motorized "parapente" on which Nicolas Hulot, the producer of "Ushuaia", rose in the air just behind the old mission to the great delight of the children.

---

[2] Wuerz Press in Winnipeg accepted to publish the manuscript and a year later *Qitdlarssuaq: The Story of a Polar Migration* was printed.

On May 22, Father went to Lennoxville, near Sherbrooke, to join the Hudson Bay Diocese group gathered at the Franciscan Monastery for the annual retreat. Pentecost Sunday, with a few confrères, he visited the historic Benedictine Abbey of Saint-Benoît-du-Lac, enjoying the peace and the beauty of the scenery.

Later in Ottawa, he was interviewed by two journalists from Europe 1 for the programme *"Bleu nature"*, directed by Nicolas Hulot. On this occasion, he made a very pertinent remark. "Even if during the interviews, we try to say what we consider important, the interviewers are the only ones responsible for the final text submitted to the public and we end up being the losers!"

Really, the media gave him no peace. British television had come in the spring. Now, a team from the Japanese television awaited him when he returned to Pond Inlet on June 14. All the interviews were of course in English. He did not mind but still felt more at home in French. Early in July, he welcomed his grand-niece Bénédicte Laurent who came from Nantes, France. Bénédicte enjoyed her visit immensely. A licensee in History, to obtain her masters degree, she would write a memoir on the Inuit Catholic Mission. And what better mentor could she find than "Tonton Guy"? Under her uncle's guidance, she easily found enough material to submit a pertinent article to the French magazine *"Famille Chrétienne"* (Christian Family), a well illustrated article. While recognizing the influence of the religion on the Inuit, Bénédicte noted that the faith of the Eskimos was still very new and for some was somewhat superficial. She wondered for instance, if the presence at Church of certain individuals was not a way of pleasing the missionary rather than a gesture inspired by a profound religious conviction?

In January 1991, Father Mary went to Quebec to visit Father Steinmann who had been advised by doctors that he had only six months to live. Consumed by cancer, he died on July 20. To the memory of his good friend, a man who left his mark wherever he went, Father Rousselière wrote a long article in *Eskimo*, N° 43, Spring-Summer 1992. Another confrère, Father Hubert Mascaret, had died a year earlier. Fathers Steinmann and Mascaret had both been sent to the northern missions the same year as Father Rousselière.

Back in Ottawa, as former recipient, he attended the presentation of the Northern Science Award to an Inuk of Povungnituk, Tamusi Qumak, author of an Inuktitut Dictionary and a study on Eskimo customs written in syllabic characters, Qumak spoke no other language than Inuktitut.

At Pond Inlet, in March, he gave the hospitality of the old mission to three Belgian adventurers who had skied the previous year through the Spitzberg and were now set to ski across Baffin Land as far as Igloolik towing all their equipment on a sled. Father Mary-Rousselière and Alain Maktar indicated to them on the map the best route to take but they went astray and lengthened their journey by about 100 kilometres.

In July 1991, at Pond Inlet, Professor Müller-Beck of the University of Tubingen, visited with Father Mary-Rousselière the main archaeological sites of the region on board the helicopter of the Polar Continental Shelf Project. The professor was full of admiration for the country and the work of Father Mary. He decided forthwith to return the following year with some students of Tubingen but because of lack of funds, he was unable to realize his project.

In *Eskimo,* N° 42, Fall-Winter 1991-1992, Father Mary-Rousselière published a well documented article on *Aids*. An untimely distribution of condoms to the Inuk youth had released in him a well justified indignation. In the following issue, in order to clear up all misunderstandings, he addressed the criticism he had received on the subject.

On September 3, Father Mary-Rousselière was again in Montreal on his way to France. During his stay in his home country, he visited the Oblates at Pontmain as well as the Basilica of Notre-Dame de la Delivrande in Normandy, where in 1938, before leaving for Canada he had gone on pilgrimage. At Pontoise, his presence reassured his sister Béatrice who had been burglarized a few days before! Her home was the base from where he visited all his relatives.

November 4, his nephew drove him to the Roissy Airport to learn that his flight had already left one hour earlier. The next day, in the morning, the taxi, reserved the night before, got involved in an accident. They ordered another one which ran out of gasoline a few kilometres from the airport but luckily not too far from a service station and finally, he made it on time for the flight back to Canada. Flying over New Brunswick, the Captain announced that he was facing a 175 Kilometre per hour wind. All the passengers were relieved when the plane touched ground safely in Mirabel.

November 7th, he arrived at Pond Inlet. In the mail piled up during his absence at the mission, he found a telephone bill in excess of $700.00. Two Inuit who knew his personal code and who had been sent to prison in Yellowknife had found it amusing to spend time phoning long distance using Father Mary's card. Maybe they thought he was Santa Claus!

In preparation for Christmas 1991, he installed the crib on the porch of the mission, not without at first making a few repairs to the fifty year old Nativity scene. He braced the falling ear of the donkey; he fixed the oxen's horns, made a hand with bread crumbs for St. Joseph and even bought a new baby Jesus. The children were delighted!

On his return from a trip to Montreal and Ottawa in February 1992, he visited his old friend Simon Arnaviapik with whom he had travelled in 1945. Arnaviapik was really only skin and bone but was all smiles when he saw Ataata Mari coming to see him. A few days later, he died and Father attended his funeral in the Anglican Church. On May 6, another old friend, Arnatsiaq, the elder of the village passed away. He had formerly been a special constable for the Mounted Police.

On May 19, Father went down to Ottawa on his way to Winnipeg where he met the Oblates of Manitoba and Hudson Bay attending a retreat already in progress. The sermons were given by a French priest who had known Father Bazin in Dijon.

Back at Pond Inlet, in July, he opened his doors to Father Firmin Michiels, a Parish Priest of Flemish descent, who came from Winnipeg to realize his dream of camping above the Arctic Circle. At the same time, he wanted to photograph the northern flowers but the wind and the rain did not help.

On August 3, the ground was covered with snow. On the 18th, a strange ship hoisting the Hammer and Sickle, anchored in front of the hamlet. It was the *"Kapitan Klebnikov"*, a former Soviet ice-breaker arriving from Korea and Japan via Alaska. The tourists were accommodated in a five story structure built on the deck.

In autumn, the sewer pipe of the mission froze three times, a contretemps you may expect when the temperature drops low down below zero. Alerted, his friend Hermann sent Father Rousselière a heating wire that Alain and Natalino installed in 40° below zero weather. He had another contretemp, this one he did not expect. Returning from Nanisivik, he found the old mission's padlocks broken and the safe in the new mission forced opened, his Mass wine stolen and his wallet emptied! "Civilization is progressing all over the North," he wrote to Father Vandevelde, with a touch of irony. The culprit, a specialist in breaking and entering, had been apprehended immediately by the Corporal of the local R.C.M.P. Still, Father Mary was without wine!

In April 1993, in the United States, Elmer Harp, professor of archaeology at Dartmouth College in Hanover, New Hampshire, had his 80th birthday. At the celebration organized by the Smithsonian Institute in his honour, all his octogenarian friends were personally invited, among them Graham Rowley and Guy Mary-Rousselière. On April 29, they left Ottawa by car with Bryan Gordon at the wheel. They went through the State of Vermont and found the scenery simply magnificent. Scientists from Denmark and three Inuit were also present at the feast, among them, George Qulaut that Father had baptized long ago at *Alarniq*, near Igloolik, where he was excavating. Everyone regretted the absence of Eigil Knuth who, in spite of his 90 years, was preparing an expedition to the North shore of Greenland and had sent his regrets.

Early May, he returned to Pond Inlet where much to his surprise he found Father Wieslaw Krotki, better known as Tony, and Sister Edith Grenier who had arrived from Igloolik by skidoo with some Inuit families. After a few days, visiting and resting, Sister Edith flew back to Igloolik. Tony together with the Inuit returned home by skidoo via Arctic Bay and Nanisivik. The weather was ideal for the trip.

Later in the month, Father Rousselière flew down to Calgary for the annual meeting of the personnel of the Churchill-Hudson Bay Diocese. On a free day, he went by bus to Edmonton to visit the French Oblates, among them Father Jean Colas, a confrère from the novitiate that he had not seen for 55 years and Father Léonce Dehurtevent who at 82 years of age was ready the next day to go back to Paulatuk on the Arctic Coast. He also met Father Robert Paradis, former missionary of the Hudson Bay Diocese who because of partial blindness had chosen to stay in St Albert. Leaving Calgary, he stopped at St. Catharines, Ontario and visited the Steltners and their friends Hans Engelund Kristiansen and his wife. He found them translating in Danish and Greenlandic his book on the Migration. For her part, Sophie Steltner was doing the same in German. The University of Tubingen had agreed to publish the manuscript.

Sunday, July 26, Father Rousselière back in Mittimatalik, heard of the tragedy when an eight year old girl was killed by hungry dogs. Her sister saw the tragedy and screamed for help but too late. The little girl did not survive. Of course, all the dogs involved in the attack were shot by the Police.

In August, Father Mary-Rousselière visited a few archaeological sites by helicopter with Professor Müller-Beck. On September 2, he left from Mirabel for Roissy-Paris. He was surprised—and pleased—to find on the plane, J. F. LeMouël who had just been excavating in the Western Arctic.

In France, near Laval, he located the properties that had given the names to his ancestors, Davière and Rousselière. He also visited Our Lady of Avesnière Basilica where many of his ancestors had been buried in the chancel, joined later by fourteen priests beheaded during the Revolution.

Invited by the group of Dijonnais who had visited Pond Inlet in June, he stopped at Dijon and was overjoyed to meet the relatives of Father Bazin known as "Oncle Étienne", the founder of Pond Inlet Mission whose companion he had been for a year. Evidently, he took photos, but alas, with an empty camera! "Zut"!

18

SAINT LAZARE STATION

On September 30, he boarded the train at Saint Lazare Station for Pontoise. "It is there", he wrote, "that my Nemesis awaited me. Wanting to arrive at my sister's before eight o'clock, I hurried down the stairs of the subway, my suitcase in hand. What happened after that, I could not tell you. The only recollection that I have is that I felt the edge of every stair pass at full speed under my nose before landing face first at the bottom of the stairwell. In fact, it was my four upper front teeth that bore the main brunt, with the nose and forehead naturally...The firemen arrived quickly and brought me to the hospital where after a anti-tetanus shot, a woman doctor sewed up my left eyebrow, the top of my nose and the left nostril". Two hours later, he arrived at his sister's, his face all bruised. But the accident did not make him change his plans. On October 29, still carrying marks from his fall, he took the plane back to Canada.

In Montreal, looking at the expression on the face of his dentist, he understood that the state of his mouth was not great. Two hours of work and another appointment did not prevent him leaving for Ottawa where as usual I picked him up at the Voyageur terminal and drove him to Deschâtelets. At the Museum of Civilization, he brought the finishing touches to the book he was ready to publish on his archaeological achievements. He counted on Dr. Jacques Cinq-Mars to provide editorial input and select the proper illustrations. He took great pleasure in talking to his friends at the Museum about his plans for the summer 1994 excavations at *Nunguvik* and *Arnakadlak.*

The Twilight

But, alas, the Lord had other plans for him which did not tally with his own! He spent Christmas at Pond Inlet, very busy preparing the 50th anniversary issue of *Eskimo* magazine. He had barely time to take fresh air and on the rare times that he ventured outside, he had to protect his face from the cold with a woolen balaklava. "It is strange", he wrote to his friends the Scullions, "since my accident, when I blow my nose, I have the impression that it is someone else's nose!" At the beginning of 1994, he came down to Montreal to see his dentist. In Ottawa he examined a new photocopier but he did not buy it. He left me the pleasure of sending it to him, courtesy of Dr. Hans Müller-Beck, passing through Ottawa en route for Pond Inlet on March 23. He installed it in April at the time Father Gérard Laprise was visiting him. "His counsel helped me", he wrote from Mittimatalik on April 12. And between brackets, he added "isn't he after all a general counsellor?", as if to say: could a counsellor do anything else but counsel? He was never to use his new acquisition.

Dr. Müller-Beck found Father Mary in good health and three days later came back to Ottawa delighted by his short visit and the welcome he received at Pond Inlet. He brought down with him a few reproductions in epoxy of archaeological specimens executed by the Inuit initiated to the art of modelling by Nina G. Zaitseva, a sympathetic

Guy Mary-Rousselière in his office (Photo Gérard Kenney—1994)

Russian lady. Father Mary-Rousselière had brought his contribution to the programme subsidized by Hermann Steltner and the University of Tubingen by showing students photos of their ancestors and demonstrating how to link the present to the past so as to face the future with enthusiasm.

As usual, on April 22, he went to bed late. Lost in reading, he forgot the time. At 11:41 p.m. he remembered that he was supposed to fax me the itinerary of his future travel for May and June 1994. He knew he could count on me to be his chauffeur from the airport to the museum and vice-versa. He asked for small wooden crosses to offer to the two children who were making their first communion on Ascension day. Then realizing that being from Belgium, I could be interested by my compatriots' exploits, he added: "My two Belgian visitors of 1991 left for the North Pole on March 5. They sent me a postcard from Ward Hunt Island. They say that I am responsible for their departure; I had told them to hurry because of the "green house effect!" Ataata Mari never did lose his sense of humour.

On December 15, 1976, after the recent fire which had destroyed the Pelly Bay Church and the Pond Inlet Co-operative, he wrote to his relatives and friends: "For me who has lived 30 years without a fire extinguisher, fire has become an obsession, for I think especially of my notes, photos and books that could not be replaced." Was this a premonition?

April 23, 1994 at 2:30 a.m., the Sacred Heart Mission of Pond Inlet was on fire. The flames could be seen from neighbouring houses. Voluntary firemen rushed to the mission but it was too late. Around 9:00 a.m. a telephone call advised me that Father Mary-Rousselière was dead, burned to death in his own living quarters.

The news of the tragedy travelled rapidly. His friend John Scullion, retired at Carleton Place, was so affected that he had a heart attack and died the following day. He was 61 years old. Father Guy's sister, Béatrice, was stunned when informed by phone of the tragic event. Because of her age, she was unable to come to Pond Inlet for the funeral. Her two daughters represented her. Father Mary had asked to be buried at the place of his death. April 30, Marie-Renée Timberlake of England and Geneviève Janet of France, "Tonton Guy's" two nieces arrived in Pond Inlet in the company of Monseigneur Rouleau. The Bishop was deeply stricken by the unexpected death of one of his missionaries. A house can be rebuilt but a man of Father Mary-Rousselière's stature cannot be replaced.

On May 4, 1994, late at night, the body was finally brought back from Toronto where an autopsy had taken place. Father, according to the experts, had died asphyxiated by the smoke rather than burned. The funeral ceremony began around 10:00 p.m. in the Anglican Church filled by Inuit. Monseigneur Rouleau presided, accompanied at the altar by Fathers Robert Lechat and Joseph Meeùs as well as catechists Thomas and Agatha Kublu, who came from Igloolik. After mass, the funeral procession moved towards the cemetery, surrounded by a cold pale light. The coffin was then slowly lowered into the tomb. A last prayer was said. The *Salve Regina* was sung. It is the farewell song to any Oblate who passes away and is entrusted to the Virgin Mary. Around 1:00 a.m., the crowd dispersed after a last adieu to Ataata Mari, Father Guy Mary-Rousselière. A humble wooden cross and a few flowers, soon blighted by frost, marked his grave.

On May 5, in the evening, right after the arrival of *First Air* in Ottawa, the Bishop, the two nieces of Father Guy and many friends attended a commemorative service held in the Seminary chapel on Main Street. Bishop Rouleau, Dr. Graham Rowley and other personalities of the Museum of Civilization rendered homage to the dear departed.

On May 6, Marie-Renée and Geneviève boarded the plane for home, their hearts heavy with sorrow but nevertheless, happy to have felt all the affection that surrounded their uncle. They were impatient to relate to their families the unforgettable days they had just experienced. They had perceived clearly the profound emptiness that the sudden death of their uncle left among Inuit and Oblates of the Churchill-Hudson Bay Diocese, but also the true consolation that faith in the resurrection might bring to believers.

On May 7, 1994, in the Notre Dame de Pontoise church, during a memorial service for Father Mary-Rousselière, emotion was very intense among his relatives and friends. Jean-François LeMouël, of the French Archaeological Mission of the Arctic, pronounced an eulogy extolling the qualities and realizations of the missionary priest and archaeologist. He compared his friend Father Mary to a tireless traveller, filled with a delicate and discreet attention for others, returning to the house of the Father. He was among the *Innumarit,* the men of excellence, a gentle, generous, humble, discreet man. He was an ethnologist gifted with an acute sense of observation, speaking the language of the natives, a specialist of Arctic Pre-history, always and everywhere at the service of the Inuit, these perpetual nomads now finally settled in villages. But above all, Father Mary-Rousselière was a priest; a serene priest celebrating mass in the small tent of *Nunguvik* accompanied by the music of the Northern wind. J. F. Le Mouël called it *"The Mass on the World".* The orator concluded with these words: "Go, Father, the Mass is ended. He who will love passionately Jesus hidden in the power that makes the Earth grow, Earth, like a mother, will lift him up in its giant arms, and will make him contemplate the face of God."

Condolences did not cease to arrive. Madame Aline Chrétien, in her name and that of The Right Honourable Jean Chrétien, Prime Minister of Canada; Peter Ernerk and Marius Tungilik in the name of the Inuit organizations they represent; Father Gérard Laprise in the name of Father Marcello Zago, Superior General of the Oblates in Rome and so many others too long to mention.

Father Guy Mary-Rousselière—Ataata Mari—a gentleman, a beloved brother and uncle, a scholar, a priest, a fellow Oblate and friend to the Inuit will be remembered with respect and admiration for a unique legacy of contributions to his Church and to all those who seek to deepen their understanding of Inuit culture. Through his published accounts, audio-visual endeavours, archaeological and ethnological projects he has left something beautiful for the North he loved so fervently.

Thanks to the efforts of Bishop Rouleau, Father Lechat, Lorraine Brandson and Philippa Ootoovak a number of documents and pictures were recovered from the burned-out structure that was almost totally consumed by fire, water and smoke damage. Many precious items including oral history recordings, a rare Arctic book collection and important files located in the desk and computer did not survive or were not salvageable. Most of the charred files and images recovered from the safe were relocated to the Eskimo Museum. Archaeological reports relating to the Pond Inlet region have been donated to the local library, *The Rebecca Idlout Library.* A copy of Father Mary's manuscript on the prehistory of Pond Inlet remains in the care of the Canadian Museum of Civilization awaiting publication.

The old mission renovated. (Photo by Joseph Meeüs, o.m.i.)

Three friends—three graves: Hermann Steltmer, Guy Mary-Rousselière and John Scullion
(Photo Joseph Meeüs, o.m.i.)

The official investigation led by the R.C.M.P. blamed the fire at the Pond Inlet mission on a short circuit provoked by an electrical heating appliance. The wire in the sacristy cupboard overheated and priestly vestments that were there burst into flames.

Since this tragic event, the mission trailer has been demolished. The old mission came out of oblivion. It was relocated, then enlarged. Once again, Pond Inlet has a prayer house for the Inuit and a shelter for travelling missionaries. The altar piece painted by Father Rousselière in 1945 has been preserved. Christ, with arms extended in a circle of light continues to reign over the mountains and draws to Himself "les Hommes par excellence", the Inuit.

At the cemetery, Ataata Mary has been joined by two of his best friends. The caskets containing the ashes of John Scullion and Hermann Steltner have been placed one on his right, the other on his left. Like him, they sincerely loved the Inuit and their culture. May the three of them rest in peace and may "Mass on Top of the World" continue!

Tagvauvutit aksualuk, Ataata Mari!

Charles Choque, o.m.i.

LIST OF NAMES (INUIT)

LIST OF NAMES (WHITES)

INUKTITUT GLOSSARY

Abvajar (Abvadyar, Abadjak, Abadya, Abadyar):	small island at the N.W. extremity of the Melville Peninsula.
Aglu:	seal's breathing hole kept open through the ice.
Ajukirtuyi:	the Anglican Minister, *the one who teaches*.
Akkilasarjuk:	at the mouth of the Prince River on the north shore of Baker Lake.
Akpa:	murre
Alarnerk (alaniq):	site south of Igloolik favourable to excavations.
Amaut:	place of the baby in the hood of the woman's parka
Angmaraluit:	a place with many openings
Areak:	Simpson Lake, 30 km long.
Arnakadlak:	archaeological site close to Nunguvik.
Arviat:	Eskimo Point, *a place where you find Greenland whales*.
Arvilidjuarmiut:	people of Pelly Bay.
Arviliqjuat (Arviligjuar):	Pelly Bay
Ataata:	father
Ataata Mari:	Father Mary-Rousselière
Atiq:	the name
Awatarpait:	seal oil skins.

Awatarpivik:	island close to the Pelly Bay Mission.
Eqaluit:	Pré-Dorset site at the bottom of Tay Sound.
Ibyo (ibjuq):	mud used on the sled runners.
Igluluarjuit:	camp in the Pond Inlet region.
Ikirtak:	lake between Pond Inlet and Igloolik
Ikpiarjuk:	bag, pocket—name given to Igloolik
Iksirardjuarapik:	Pope—the very High Priest.
Innumarit:	the super-men.
Inuktorvik:	a lake—*where someone ate human flesh*—close to some deposits.
Inusiq:	the life
Iqaluit:	Frobisher Bay, the Capital of Nunavut.
Irkalulik:	*—where there is fish*—lake close to Pelly Bay good for fall fishing.
Isortok:	lake long and narrow south of Pelly Bay.
Kaggik:	the big igloo for meetings or celebrations.
Kairnirmiut (Qairnirmiut):	people of Baker Lake.
Kakiwak:	three-pronged fish spear.
Kalâtdlit:	Greenlanders.
Kanayurtuq:	location in the Pond Inlet region.
Kangik:	the camp where Monica Attaguttaluk passed away.
Kangiqsujuaq:	Wakeham Bay, Nunavik (Québec)
Kapuivik:	Inuit camp on Jens Munk Island.
Kayak (qajaq):	hunting boat of the Inuit.
Kayualuk:	inuktitut surname of Father Pierre Henry because of his red beard.
Kayukuluk:	name of Father Danielo (the little red beard).

Kolliktar (qullitak):	outer caribou skin parka worn the hair outside.
Krikirtarjuk:	small island. Place in the Igloolik region with some Dorsetian remains.
Kudliq (qulliq):	stone lamp using seal or whale oil; also the Primus stove.
Kugarjuk (Kugaardjuk):	The big river flowing in the bay of Pelly.
Kunguardjuk:	part of the Kur River good for fall fishing, 50 km from Pelly Bay.
Kurluktuq:	waterfall in the Milne Inlet region.
Kursluk:	—*the bad river*—between Repulse Bay and Pelly Bay.
Maktaq:	skin of white whale considered as a delicacy.
Nadlua:	archaeological site in Navy Board Inlet.
Nanisivik:	Strathcona mine.
Nanualuk:	a big bear (Nanuk :bear; aluk : big).
Nauyat:	Repulse Bay—*the place of the seagulls*.
Netchilik: (Nattiliq or Netjilik)	Inuit de la région de Pelly Bay *where there are seals.*
Niaqongut:	excavation site in the Pond Inlet region.
Nirlirnartok:	a place where one finds geese.
Nunasiar:	a small mission built by Ataata Mari, west of Pond Inlet.
Nunguvik:	main archaeological site close to Nadlua.
Nutarasungniq:	place between Button Point and Pond Inlet.
Padlirmiut (Pallirmiut):	Inuit of the Padlei region, close to the tree limit.
Pingerkalik :	camp in the Igloolik region.

Qallunaat:	White Men.
Qamanittuaq:	Baker Lake (a lake with a river running right through)
Qinnibvik:	location of Arnaviapik's camp.
Saatut:	archaeological site, west at the entrance of Navy Board Inlet.
Sanerajak (Sanirajak):	Hall Beach.
Sanningayuligmiut:	Inuk living on Garry Lake.
Sapputit:	fish weirs.
Sarvartormiut:	people of the Kazan.
Siksik:	kind of ground squirrel.
Siurarjuk:	place in the Igloolik region, a place where there is sand.
Tarniq:	the soul
Tassiqjuar:	—*the large lake*—around 20 kms from Pelly Bay.
Tassiuyark:	a place with some resemblance to a lake (tassiq).
Tununirmiut:	Inuit living in the Pond Inlet region.
Ugjuk:	bearded seal
Ukkusiksaligmiut:	people of the Back River. *A place rich in soapstone.*
Umiak:	boat made of skins used for hunting or transportation of families.

Études archéologiques
de Guy Mary-Rousselière

Archaeological Studies
by Guy Mary-Rousselière

1969   Exploration archéologique de la côte ouest d'Eclipse Sound et de Milne Inlet (Nord-Baffin) — Été 1969 — Rapport préliminaire.

1970   Fouilles archéologiques dans la région d'Eclipse Sound — 1970 — Rapport préliminaire.

1971   Fouilles archéologiques dans la région de Pond Inlet et d'Eclipse Sound — 1971 — Rapport préliminaire au Conseil des Arts du Canada.

1972   Report on salvage archaeological excavations at the Button Point (N.W.T.) site (PfFm-1) in 1972.

1973   Rapport au Conseil des Arts du Canada sur les fouilles archéologiques effectuées dans la région de Pond Inlet en 1973.

1974   Rapport sur les fouilles effectuées dans la région de Pond Inlet en 1974.

1975   Preliminary report on archaeological excavations in the Pond Inlet region (1975).
Rapport sur les fouilles effectuées dans la région de Pond Inlet en 1975.

1977   Preliminary report on archaeological excavations at Nunguvik, Navy Board Inlet (1977).
Rapport sur les fouilles archéologiques effectuées dans la région d'Eclipse Sound en 1977.

1978   Preliminary report on archaeological research in the Pond Inlet region in 1978.

1979   Preliminary report on archaeological excavations at Nunguvik (Navy Board Inlet) (1979).

1980   Preliminary report on archaeological excavations in the Navy Board Inlet-Eclipse Sound region, N.W.T. Fouilles archéologiques à Nunguvik et à Saatut (Nord Baffin) en 1980.

1981   Preliminary report on aechaeological research in the Navy Board Inlet- Eclipse Sound region, Summer 1981.

1982   Preliminary report on archaeological excavations in the Navy Board Inlet-Eclipse Sound region, 1982. Summary of archaeological field work at Nunguvik and Saatut in 1982.

1983   Preliminary report on archaeological excavations Navy Board Inlet — Summer 1983. Interim report on the Navy Board Inlet sites: discovery of sites and chronology of archaeological work (c. 1983).

1984   Preliminary report on archaeological excavations in Navy Board Inlet — Summer 1984.

1985   Report on archaeological excavations at Nunguvik and Arnakadlak sites (Navy Board Inlet) (1985).

1986   Preliminary report on archaeological excavations in Navy Board Inlet (Summer 1986).

1987   Preliminary report on archaeological investigations in Navy Board Inlet (Summer 1987).

1989   Preliminary report on archaeological work in the Pond Inlet region, 1989. Archaeological investigations in the Navy Board Inlet and Eclipse Sound area, 1989. Correspondence — J. Meldgaard, Denmark. Correspondence — National Museum Ottawa. Government permits.

Igloolik 1954 - Pelly Bay - Radio — review — Repulse Bay.

Reconnaissance archéologique dans la région de Pond Inlet, T.N.O.

Remarks on some types of Pre-Dorset and Dorset harpoon heads.

Santa Fe conference 1972 - The Palaeo-Eskimo in Northern Baffin Island.

Miscellaneous (2 files).

Livres — Articles — Books

Beyond the High Hills
— royalty reports
— correspondence — The World Publishing Co.

Eskimo voyages in Northern Canada
— Scott Polar Inst. 1969
— carbon copy of article submitted.

Exploration and Evangelization of the Canadian North 1981.

Handbook of North American Indians — chapter on Iglulik Eskimos.
— correspondence with Dr. David Damas — early 1980s.

How Monica Ataguttaaluk Initiated me to Arctic Arthaeology
Inuktitut — spring 1987.

Inculturation? D'accord... Mais jusqu'où?
Kerygma — 1985.

Jeux de ficelle
— correspondence - National Museum of Man.
— string figures - National Museum of Man.

Qitdlarssuaq
— corrections — English — publisher
— correspondence — book reviews, comments
— genealogy — Greenland — Qitdlarssuaq book
— migration — Inuit testimony
— migration — Greenland — misc.research
— research notes — mainly book references (2 files).

(Compilation: Lorraine Brandson —
Eskimo museum — Churchill, MB.)

Eskimo Magazine
Articles by Guy Mary-Rousselière
in Chronological order
from 1947 to 1993

Printed in Canada

 **Transcontinental
Printing Inc.**
MÉTROLITHO DIVISION